INTRODUCTORY ESSAYS ON *EGILS SAGA* AND *NJÁLS SAGA*

Edited by

JOHN HINES AND DESMOND SLAY

VIKING SOCIETY FOR NORTHERN RESEARCH

LONDON

All contributions copyright the authors. ISBN 0 903521 25 3

Printed at Oxford University Computing Services, 1992

Foreword

In the earlier 1980s, the Viking Society for Northern Research extended its involvement in promoting the university study of Old Norse literature and related topics by launching a series of annual Student Conferences at which lecturers and students could gather for talks and seminars that were able to range beyond what could normally be catered for in a university timetable in terms both of scope and of variety. In the course of time, a perception has grown that some of the material presented at these meetings not only merits more than a fleeting public appearance but could also help to redress a shortage of helpful, introductory critical reading in English on central texts in the study of Old Norse. The Viking Society accepted a proposal to publish, in an inexpensive and informal form, papers from the Student Conferences held in Cardiff in 1988 and London in 1990, which had concentrated on *Egils saga Skalla-Grímssonar* and *Brennu-Njáls saga* respectively. One of these papers, Rory McTurk's, has already been published in *Saga-Book* XXIII(1) (1990), 28-45. Guðrún Nordal's essay on the historical circumstances in which these sagas emerged was specially written for this volume. To compensate in part for the sporadic appearance of references and scholarly footnoting in this book — material that is not at home in the text of a clear and direct lecture — bibliographical guides to published work on each of these sagas have been provided at the end.

Thanks are due to the Viking Society, for its support for this volume, and to the contributors for their co-operation in the task of reproducing their talks in printed form. Particular thanks are due to Peter Robinson, at the Oxford University Computing Services, for his efforts in converting the contributors' various computer disks to a common format.

John Hines, March 1992

Contents

Sturlunga saga and the context of saga-writing

Guðrún Nordal
Department of Scandinavian Studies
University College London

Sturlunga saga is a compilation of sagas that relate contemporary events in Iceland in the twelfth and thirteenth centuries, the period in which the writers of the family sagas lived. The saga is not only an important source of historical information, but also provides a valuable insight into the viewpoints and ideals of thirteenth-century Icelanders.

The genesis of *Sturlunga saga* not only sheds light on the writing of sagas in the thirteenth century, but also bears witness to attitudes to these sagas at the end of that period. The making of *Sturlunga* is marked by two distinct stages: the writing of each of the twelve sagas — short and long — during the course of the thirteenth century and the integration and editing of these sagas into one work, *Sturlunga saga*, around 1300. The name of the compilation, which is first quoted in a seventeenth century source, is derived from the most powerful family in the thirteenth century, the Sturlungs. The final period of the Icelandic Commonwealth, from the late twelfth century to its fall in 1262, is also known as the *Sturlung Age*.

The sagas in *Sturlunga* were written over a period of a hundred years up to 1300, the same period as that in which many of the family sagas were composed. The family sagas and the sagas in *Sturlunga* are related in two important ways: they share their subject matter, that is, broadly speaking, stories about Icelanders in the Commonwealth period, and, again broadly speaking, they have the same date of composition. But even though the authors of many of the family sagas and of *Sturlunga saga* were contemporaries, they had a very different perspective on the events they purport to represent. The closeness of the authors of

Sturlunga to the events they interpret restrained them in their treatment of the historical material, while the authors of the family sagas had artistic freedom to re-work old stories about Icelanders in the ninth and tenth centuries. However this closeness to events gives an acute sense of urgency to the descriptions of acts of terror, fights and sorrows in *Sturlunga* that is not felt in the family sagas.

Snorri Sturluson and *Egils saga*
Some of the stories of Icelanders in the family sagas and in the shorter *Íslendingaþættir* reflect the tension that there was in the relationship between Iceland and the royal court in Norway in the thirteenth century. Egill Skalla-Grímsson's battles with the court are perhaps the best known example of an Icelander's obstinate resistance to the rulings of the Norwegian king. The saga of Egill can be attributed with some probability to Snorri Sturluson (1179-1241), a man who himself had a complex relationship with the Norwegian king, Hákon Hákonarson (1217-63). When Snorri Sturluson was in Norway in 1218-20 he preferred to stay with Earl Skúli, the King's Regent, rather than with the young King. On his return to Iceland Snorri wrote the poem *Háttatal*, which is preserved as part of his *Edda*. The poem was intended to be a eulogy for Hákon and Skúli, but the praise Snorri chooses for Hákon comes close to being 'háð en eigi lof' (mockery not praise). On a later visit to Norway, in 1237, Snorri again chose to support his friend Earl Skúli in his struggle with the King for supremacy. Skúli's treason was violently punished when he was killed by the King's men in 1240. A year later, Snorri was brutally murdered at Reykjaholt at the instigation of Gizurr Þorvaldsson, who was then acting on the orders of the King. Snorri's death was thus a reflection of the King's growing involvement in Icelandic affairs, particularly after 1235.

In spite of Snorri's interest in courtly splendour and royalty, evident both in *Heimskringla*, his history of the Norwegian kings, and in his court poetry dedicated to foreign dignitaries, he did not support the growing party in favour of a Norwegian conquest of Iceland in the thirteenth century. Snorri was in Norway when the Norwegians were planning to attack Iceland in 1220. He managed to dissuade them by convincing the Earl and the King not only of his support for the King but also of his ability to persuade and influence the Icelandic chieftains, which he promised to employ in the King's interest. Snorri did not, however, fulfil his promise on his return to Iceland.

If we accept that Snorri wrote *Egils saga*, he probably did so in his later years when he had become disillusioned with the Norwegian King. Our knowledge of Snorri Sturluson and other chieftains in Iceland in the thirteenth century is primarily drawn from two contemporary sagas of the thirteenth century written by his nephew, Sturla Þórðarson: from *Hákonar saga Hákonarsonar*, and above all from *Íslendinga saga*, which is preserved as the greater part of the *Sturlunga saga* compilation. Writing about contemporary events did not allow for formal introductions of characters, and little attempt is made to connect figures of the thirteenth century with saga heroes. It is therefore curious that Egill Skalla-Grímsson, who was Snorri Sturluson's forefather, appears in an episode in *Íslendinga saga*, when Snorri is planning to move from his farm Borg á Mýrum (also Egill's farm) to Reykjaholt. Snorri's *ráðsmaðr* (housemaster), Egill Halldórsson, is visited by Egill Skalla-Grímsson in a dream:

> Egill dreamt that Egill Skalla-Grímsson came to him and was frowning greatly. He said: "Does our kinsman Snorri intend to leave this place?" "So men say," said Egill. "He intends to go away, and in that he does ill," says the dream-figure, "because seldom have men ruled over us Mýrarmen when we prospered, nor need he scorn this land". Then he spoke a verse:
>
> > Men now spare to strike with a sword;
> > blood looks snow-white;
> > we look towards an age of scourges;
> > sharp blade won land for me,
> > sharp blade won land for me.
> > (Ch.16: *ca.*1205 AD)

Sturla Þórðarson's portrayal of Snorri Sturluson in *Íslendinga saga* has this dream at its roots. Snorri is criticised not only for want of bravery, but also for a greed and an avarice which were seen as the flaws of character responsible for Snorri's failure in human relationships, particularly with his kinsmen. The verse given to Egill Skalla-Grímsson here sharpens Sturla's criticism of his uncle, and has even greater significance if Snorri were the author of *Egils saga*.

When Snorri was murdered in 1241, the King's involvement in Icelandic affairs could no longer be withstood. The King successfully manipulated ambitious young Icelandic chieftains, and contracted them to 'koma landinu undir sik', 'bring the land under his sway'. He fuelled their ambitions and enmities, with the result that the civil war which raged in Iceland from c.1235 could only be resolved by his intervention. The King acted in accordance with prevailing sentiments of the time, as echoed by Cardinal William from Sabina in 1247, when he visited Norway to crown King Hákon: 'he thought it improbable that this country would not serve a king as all others in the world did.' Fifteen years later, King Hákon had gained power over Iceland, and Gizurr Þorvaldsson, the instigator of Snorri's murder, became the first Earl of Iceland.

The writing of a contemporary saga
The most extensive source describing the actions of men and women during the last decades of the Icelandic Commonwealth is *Íslendinga saga*. Its author, Sturla Þórðarson was one of six illegitimate childen of Þóra and Þórðr Sturluson, Snorri's brother. Þórðr was the eldest son of Sturla Þórðarson, the old chieftain of the Sturlung family. *Íslendinga saga* focusses upon the activities of its author's kinsmen and the dramatic events that closely affected that family. Sturla had the difficult task of writing contemporary history, and both the scope of the saga and the closeness of the events forced him to select his material carefully. Yet he did not limit himself to a single biography; he set himself the ambitious task of telling the history of Iceland in the thirteenth century, attempting to create a coherent structure out of the chaos and havoc that characterises the period.

Íslendinga saga is the longest section of *Sturlunga saga*, and is of immense value in the comparative study of the different types of sagas written in the thirteenth century. It is the only saga about Icelandic events for which we know not only the author's name, but also his social standing and background. Sturla Þórðarson probably started writing *Íslendinga saga* in the last years of his life, after he had written *Hákonar saga Hákonarsonar* and the now lost *Magnúsar saga lagabætis*. *Íslendinga saga* opens by documenting the death of Sturla Þórðarson in 1183. The subject matter of the first part of the saga, and that of the other sagas in *Sturlunga saga* which concern themselves with events up to 1235, is similar to that of the family sagas. Feuds arise from personal enmities, over financial disputes or because of women, and are settled locally. After 1235 the focus of the saga shifts from the petty harshnesses of local life to the political transformation of the country. This break in the saga coincides with the attempt of one Sturla Sighvatsson (the author's cousin) to bring Iceland under the Norwegian throne, an enterprise frustrated by the rise to power of Gizurr Þorvaldsson.

Sturla Þórðarson organised the complicated material at hand by distinguishing Sturla Sighvatsson and Gizurr Þorvaldsson from other actors on the scene by mentioning their birth and namegiving, and by sketching a brief scene from their adolescence which foreshadows their mature life. Their lives are to be regarded as running parallel, the one to highlight the other, even though their paths do not cross until late in Sturla Sighvatsson's life. The downfall of one is the victory of the other. Gizurr Þorvaldsson killed Sturla Sighvatsson in a battle at Örlygsstaðir in 1238. He hit his enemy, who was in no state to defend himself: 'Gizurr leapt up with both feet when he hit Sturla, so that the air could be seen between his feet and the ground' (Ch.138). His immense hatred is illuminated by the power invested in this blow. Sturla's father, Sighvatr, and two of Sturla's brothers, were also killed in the battle. Gizurr achieved Sturla's ambition twenty-four years later, when he became the first Earl of Iceland in 1262.

To call a saga 'contemporary' means that it tells the story of events that happened in the near past, and that its author is therefore in a position to draw on his own

experience or fresh eyewitness accounts. It is almost as if
this closeness to events forces the author of *Íslendinga saga*
into the background. Sturla often describes his own
experience in the saga but rarely openly passes his own
judgement upon the action. However he does use literary
methods reminiscent of the family saga to guide the reader,
or the listener, of the saga to an understanding of the
significance of an event: by introducing predictions and
comments by wise men, especially his father, through
dreams and supernatural happenings before critical events,
and also through references to public opinion. His
ingenious use of verse is particularly revealing. He rarely
uses verse as a source for the narrative, but more as a
platform for opinions and views on the preceding action.
He even quotes himself. We can sense his outrage against
Kolbeinn ungi and Gizurr Þorvaldsson, who seek to
demolish the power of the Sturlung family in the years after
the battle at Örlygsstaðir, when he and his cousin, Órækja
Snorrason, are unlawfully seized:

> Now we are two — but I hardly
> expect a reliable truce.
> In troubles and sorrow I pass
> my time — in Kolbeinn's power.
> You will know that we were
> greater in numbers at Christmas.
> The shields that were carried
> in the battle reddened in the fighting.
> (Ch.157: 1242 AD)

Sturla Þórðarson lays bare his criticism of the actions
of his cousin, Sturla Sighvatsson, by quoting predictions and
omens that highlight the seriousness of Sturla's ambition.
But at one point his mask drops. Writing of the summer of
1229, only a few months after Sturla Sighvatsson's farm had
been savagely attacked by his enemies, the author forgets to
hide his admiration for his kinsman: 'he was wearing a red
cloak, and it is my opinion that few people have seen so
brave a man' (Ch.75: 1229 AD).

At times, however, he cannot refrain from
commenting on the horror of an event, particularly when
the subject affects him personally. In a 'burning' episode at

Flugumýri in which his thirteen-year-old daughter was one of the intended victims, he decribes her narrow escape from the fire with great sensitivity: 'still a child in her years, she was quite exhausted' (Ch.174: 1253 AD).

Dreams can be used to powerful effect in the family sagas, preparing the readers for imminent tragedies and/or imposing a structure upon the narrative. Sturla uses this literary device in an imaginative way in *Íslendinga saga*. Many dreams are recounted before the battle at Örlygsstaðir that create a deep sense of foreboding about the seriousness of the conflict between Sturla and Gizurr. The verses that are recited in dreams in the months preceding the battle are ominous. Through the evocation of images of Ragnarǫk and Doomsday, the audience is made aware of the fatalistic aspect of the battle. In the context of these verses, the battle at Örlygsstaðir can be interpreted as the first step on the road to the collapse of the Commonwealth. One Jón Grettisson heard the following verse, which contains vivid echoes of *Vǫluspá*, in a dream in the summer of 1238:

> Beware! Beware!
> For the wind blows high.
> Blood will rain down
> on men's naked bodies.
> Point and edge will share
> the inheritance of men,
> now that the sword-age
> has dawned upon us

(Ch. 136)

The thirteenth century as a context for saga-writing

By comparing some details of the burning at Flugumýrr in *Íslendinga saga* and the burning of Njáll in *Njáls saga* we can highlight some of the characteristics of the contemporary saga. Each burning forms the second climax in its saga. The killing of Sturla Sighvatsson at Örlygsstaðir is the first climax in *Íslendinga saga*; the killing of Gunnarr Hámundarson is the first in *Njáls saga*. In *Njáls saga* the burners avenge the killing of Hǫskuldr Hvítanessgoði: in *Íslendinga saga*, however, they are motivated by political ambitions.

Predictions and visions alert the inhabitants of Bergþórshváll to the impending tragedy. Their uneasy forebodings are confirmed when news reaches the farm that Flosi Þórðarson has gathered together a group of men. As they approach the house, Njáll disregards his sons' advice to face the attackers outside and takes the fatal decision to go indoors. Frustrated by the slow progress of the assault, the attackers decide to set fire to the farm. The burning is observed from both sides: we listen to the conversation between the burners and eavesdrop on the people inside the farm.

When the building is ablaze, Flosi permits women, children and workmen to leave the burning farm. He also offers a truce to Njáll. The narrator describes only those characters that are of relevance to the saga: we see Njáll and Bergþóra deny Flosi's offer and prepare for bed under the ox-hide, taking their grandson Þórðr Kárason with them; we listen to Kári and Skarpheðinn's conversation before Kári leaves the fire; we observe Skarpheðinn's courageous mockery throughout this horrific episode. Yet the narrative is well-ordered and balanced in spite of the horror of the killing. The author of the saga stands at a distance from which he can judge the action. The bodies of Njáll and Bergþóra are found the following day under the shrivelled hide. They 'were quite unmarked by the flames'. Hjalti Skeggjason bears witness to this miracle, saying that he thinks 'Bergþóra's body is rather better preserved than could have been expected; but Njáll's countenance and body appear to have a radiance which I have never seen on a dead man before'.

With this episode in mind, we shall look at the story of the year 1253 (Chs.172-4). The burners arrive unexpectedly at Flugumýrr, in the middle of the night, only three days after the wedding of Gizurr's son Hallr to Ingibjǫrg, the daughter of Sturla Þórðarson, the author of the saga. Sturla had attended the wedding celebration but had left Flugumýrr before the burners arrived. The author is therefore relying on eyewitness account, not his own experience, even though this historical event affected him personally.

Most of the people in the farm are in bed when the attackers make their way into the farm. The attackers strike people in their beds; men wearing only their nightshirts defend themselves as best they can. A violent fight takes place inside the farmhouse. It is worth noting that no negotiations take place between the burners and the attackers, as in *Njáls saga*, whilst the fighting goes on. A few comments are offered, but otherwise the author uses indirect speech.

In *Njála* the blazing heat and smoke cause little concern, but at Flugumýrr the smoke is so stifling that Þorbjrn, fittingly called 'nef', 'the nose', afterwards remembered that he heard 'Gizurr praying to God in many ways, so passionately that he said he had never heard such prayers; but he thought he himself could not open his mouth for smoke'.

The attackers never confront Gizurr Þorvaldsson during the fight, but the saga describes how he parts from his wife Gróa: 'because he thought that she would live but he would die ..Gizurr realised that Gróa was greatly upset by their parting'. She did not survive the fire, however, and 'some men say that Þorsteinn genja shoved Gróa into the fire'. The horror is not disguised. No-one is spared.

Sturla's description of Gizurr Þorvaldsson's last defence shows Gizurr's strong urge to survive, and the depth of Sturla's story-telling. In *Íslendinga saga* the manner of the defence is of less importance than its success or failure. Gizurr Þorvaldsson's final resort in the burning at Flugumýrr is not his sword but a barrel of whey:

> They came to the barrel, when Gizurr was sitting in the barrel, and three or four men thrust their spears into the barrel. They quarrelled. Some said that something had been hit and some said not. Gizurr put his hands carefully in front of his stomach so they would not notice that they had touched something. The palms of his hands were scratched and also the bones of his legs. These were small but numerous wounds. Gizurr himself has said since that before they entered the pantry he was shaking from the cold so that ripples

were made in the barrel, but as they came into the pantry he stopped shaking.

Gizurr's poor physical state is further noted when he stumbles into the church: 'he was then so cold, that he could not stay there any longer .. the woman, who warmed him between her thighs, was named Hallfríðr and called *garðafylja* (yard-filly)'. It is remarkable that the whole portrait of Gizurr in the saga can accommodate this extraordinary episode, as indeed it stretches to depict him at all stages in his life. When the remains of the bodies of Gróa and their son Ísleifr are carried out of the burning farm, Gizurr is clearly shaken:

> Then Ísleifr Gizurarson was borne out on his shield, and there was nothing left of his body except the torso, roasted inside his byrnie. Next they discovered the breast of Gróa, and what was left of it was borne out on a shield to Gizurr. Gizurr said: 'Páll, kinsman, you may now look upon Ísleifr my son, and upon Gróa my wife'. And Páll saw that Gizurr turned away, and saw that tears started from his eyes like hailstones.

These quotations from *Íslendinga saga* underscore the characteristics of contemporary narrative. The confusion, the heat and the horror of the burning are not disguised in the narrative, but are made perfectly clear by accurate and precise descriptions. The horror of the episode is thus enhanced by minute details; yet at the same time the abundance of information about the people involved and their deaths makes the burning appear to the reader as a confused and chaotic scene. We remain outsiders as the tragedy unfolds in front of us. This way of showing, instead of telling, bluntly exposes the horror and senselessness of the burning at Flugumýrr.

Christian beliefs and syncretism in the thirteenth century
Death scenes in *Íslendinga saga* emphasise a man's need to reconcile himself with his religious beliefs, and often show him as a morally changed man. These are almost the only times in the saga where the author focusses on the inner man and his personal conscience. The man repents for his

sins and prepares for life after death. It is noteworthy that when powerful men die this pious element is particularly emphasized, even though they may not have shown any special Christian devotion in their everyday lives. Religious remorse enters into the narrative with almost rhythmic regularity: the person repents of his sins, receives the last offices from a priest and sings prayers. This emphasis on death-scenes in the narrative seems to show that the need to die at peace with God was a conventional ideal upheld in thirteenth-century Iceland.

Yet when these men are denied truce in battle their remorseful mood changes into a fighting spirit. Cowardice is always held contemptible. When Oddr Þórarinsson successfully triumphs over his enemy Hrani Koðránsson, Hrani asks to see a priest. Hrani atones for his sins, and 'all the men saw that he had been greatly touched by it; then he stood up' (Ch.179: 1254 AD). Hrani is aware of the men's reaction and says: 'It may be .. that you think that I have not reacted manfully. But I very much fear that that resting place which would be good for me is not secured.' He then resumes his defence and 'said it was up to each man to defend his own life'. He fought bravely until he was killed. There is a tension in Hrani's words between the view that one ought to be brave and courageous at death's door and the overwhelming awareness of the wrongdoings of one's life.

Some men choose to remember their worldly indulgence and the women who made their lives more pleasurable. Before he is killed, Þorgils Sveinsson, one of the men who took part in the burning at Flugumýrr, pays chivalrous tribute to the women he has known: 'may the sweet women live ... healthy and happy' (Ch.176: 1254 AD). One Þórir jökull, a follower of Sturla Sighvatsson, recites a verse before his execution at Örlygsstaðir. He is afraid of dying and feels the cold sea drizzle like a foretaste of death, but then he takes himself in hand:

> Do not cry, you bald headed man,
> even though a shower falls over you.
> You had the love of women;
> once shall every man die.   (Ch.139: 1238 AD)

This is a very moving verse. The proximity of death, and the natural fear the verse expresses, are more real here than in any of the more elaborately religious death-scenes that are to be found in *Íslendinga saga.*

There is some evidence that stories of the pagan gods had become a source of entertainment in the thirteenth century. Sturla Þórðarson tells us in *Hákonar saga* that Snorri Sturluson entertained Skúli's court by telling stories about Óðinn, and then, in a verse, compared one of Skúli's enemies who had betrayed the earl's trust with the heathen god. By this date the perception of the pagan religion had become stereotyped. Óðinn is portrayed as the archetypal breaker of oaths. The stereotyped portrayal of Freyr as the god who had sacrificed his sword for a woman is embodied in Snorri Sturluson's account of the fertility god in his *Edda,* where his main story about Freyr is the myth of Freyr's wooing of Gerðr, for whom he made the fatal sacrifice that lost him his life at Ragnarǫk.

The Christian chieftains, Sturla Sighvatsson and Gizurr Þorvaldsson, who are represented by Sturla Þórðarson as the two main players in the political course of events of thirteenth-century Iceland, are conspicuously likened to these two pagan gods in the saga: Sturla to Freyr, and Gizurr to Óðinn.

Sturla was given the nickname Dala-Freyr by his enemies Þórðr and Snorri Þorvaldssynir, who were protected and advised by their guardian Snorri Sturluson. This nickname has derogative connotations in the context of the saga, alluding to Sturla's lack of manhood, to his cowardice in battle and to his vanity. Snorri Sturluson and Sturla Sighvatsson were in conflict with one another after Sturla became a chieftain. One of the reasons for their enmity lay in Sturla's marriage to Solveig Sæmundsdóttir, a woman Snorri Sturluson had clearly intended for himself. It is likely that this extraordinary nickname can be attributed to Snorri Sturluson or his milieu, where tales of gods were told for amusement. It is therefore probable that the name not only impugned Sturla's bravery in battle, but was intended to mock his womanizing. Sturla was killed at the battle at Örlygsstaðir, which Sturla Þórðarson highlights as the Doomsday of the Commonwealth.

Sturla Sighvatsson was killed by Gizurr Þorvaldsson, whom Sturla Þórðarson compares to Óðinn in the last stanza in the saga, after Gizurr Þorvaldsson has cheated him out of power in Borgarfjörðr in the year 1262. Sturla quotes his own verse:

> Óðinn [Gizurr] has betrayed
> the wise man of all the good things
> he had promised — I am telling the truth —
> because he has cheated me.
> The cunning earl, who is lying
> — I understand what the chieftain wants:
> Gautr allowed himself to have enemies —
> he has kept me away.
>
> (Ch.197: 1261 AD)

The allusion to Gautr (Óðinn) enables Sturla to criticise Gizurr in a subtle way, but this pagan allusion, and Sturla Sighvatsson's nickname, could only be effective as assessments of aspects of their characters if the audience knew the stories of the gods. This verse is a good example of Sturla Þórðarson's control of the complexity of his saga. Through it, Sturla succinctly expresses deep personal hatred in the middle of a chapter impartially relating Gizurr's success. *Íslendinga saga* is designed to be, fundamentally, a faithful documentation of historical events, and Sturla has this means at his disposal to express two views of an event.

Conclusion

Sturla Þórðarson probably wrote *Íslendinga saga* in the last years of his life (1270-1284). He had by then outlived most of his enemies, kinsmen and friends, and the society he was born into in the year 1214 had disappeared. In *Íslendinga saga* he sought to document the reasons and motivations behind the collapse of the Icelandic Commonwealth. He probably wanted to explain that these men — such as his kinsmen and himself — were not in control of their own destinies. It was their bitter fate to live in such difficult times. His saga has a predominantly secular point of view. It is a saga of political feuds and battles, and the events are rarely seen in an explicitly Christian moral perspective. Yet the saga clearly bears witness to its author's Christianity.

Sturla Þórðarson shows admirable courage in *Íslendinga saga*. He confronts and illuminates the horrible and tragic events he had himself experienced, and describes them with truthfulness and skill. His saga is the most valuable evidence of real ethical behaviour in the thirteenth century by which we can judge actions in the family sagas. Some of the most powerful narrative sequences in *Íslendinga saga*, such as the description of the burning at Flugumýrr, demonstrate that his writing is not only important as a historical source but that at the same time it equals the finest literary achievements of the thirteenth century.

Bibliography

Edition: Jón Jóhannesson, Magnús Finnbogason and Kristján Eldjárn, eds. *Sturlunga saga*, 2 vols., Sturlunguútgáfan, Reykjavík, 1946.

Translation: Julia H. McGrew and R. George Thomas, *Sturlunga Saga*, 2 vols., Twayne Publishers Inc., New York, and The American-Scandinavian Foundation, 1970 and 1974.

Íslendinga saga appears in volume 1 of both of these publications.

Kingship in *Egils saga*

John Hines
School of English Studies
University of Wales, Cardiff.

Egils saga is a saga that is both rich and clearly structured. It is rich in having several themes which are developed in some substance in the course of the saga, and of these kingship is one. Nobody should, or perhaps ever would, claim that kingship is the central theme of the saga — that place must be taken by Egill's career, introduced and concluded by tales of his immediate ancestors and descendants — and if there is anything like a critical consensus on the purpose of the saga it is probably that view which lays most emphasis on the saga as the biography of a poet, revealing the occasions on which many fine skaldic verses were composed, and trying to paint an historical portrait of the man who composed them. However, many significant episodes in the course of the saga involve the dealings of Egill or his ancestors with a succession of kings: in particular his uncle, Þórólfr, with Haraldr Hárfagr, and Egill himself with two of Haraldr's sons, Eiríkr and Hákon, and with the English king Athelstan. This is by no means an exclusive list of the kings who have some form of contact with Egill and who play some role in the saga.

A straightforward and quite just view of the presence and function of these kings in *Egils saga* is that they create a context: they serve to elevate the sphere of action in the saga and consequently to elevate the status of other characters such as Egill's family and his friend, Arinbjǫrn, who are able or who are bold enough to stand up with them or against them. Hence Gwyn Jones writes in the introduction to his translation of the saga: "There is more at stake, and always a mightier background to the immediate action, than is customary in the sagas" and can use terms such as "splendid resistance" and "triumphant sections" in describing the saga. But no simple and functional explanation fully accounts for all the aspects of the presentation of kings in *Egils saga*. It is perfectly apparent that kings in the saga vary considerably, in character, in terms of the success and failure of their careers, and in terms of their effect on the other major characters of the saga. The case I wish to put forward in this paper is that through a study of how these kings vary we may discover elements of a consistent and comprehensible attitude to kingship. We may discover what look like conscious and sub-conscious social ideals intrinsic to the composition of the saga, and describe an effective literary exploitation of these attitudes and ideals.

We can very reasonably predict of this saga that at heart the attitude to *Norwegian* kingship at least should be consistent with what appears to have been a standardized medieval Icelandic view of 9th- and 10th-century Norwegian and Icelandic history, such as is effectively enunciated by Ari Þorgilsson in his *Libellus Islandorum* (*Íslendingabók*). This is an explanatory account of history which sees the Norse settlement of Iceland as largely the result of the reaction of independently-minded Norsemen to the extension of the royal power of Haraldr Hárfagr over all of Norway — the historical context in which *Egils saga* opens. Ari's severely selective and decisively organized history includes further instances of conflicts of interest between Icelanders and Norwegian kings which amount to threats posed by the kings: the ban and subsequent tax on travel 'out' from Norway for fear of the depopulation of the kingdom, and the menacing posture of Óláfr Tryggvason in the story of the conversion of Iceland to Christianity. But here, in fact, we have the essence of a paradox or dilemma: Óláfr Tryggvason's aggressive interference may be resented, but for Ari, and established opinion in 13th-century Iceland, the introduction of Christianity must be seen as a Good Thing. Kings of Norway could be beneficial. I believe that there is a similar division of attitude towards Norwegian kings in *Egils saga*. Attitudes towards these kings in the saga may be argued to vary according to a conflict between a traditional historical hostility — perhaps 'suspicion' would be a better word — towards the Norwegian kingship, and aspects of a very real dependency upon the fulfilment of the kingly role, primarily in the saga narrative, but by extrapolation also in the society of 13th-century Iceland. In broad terms it is Haraldr Hárfagr who functions most predictably in terms of the model of historical understanding which I have just outlined. The saga reader is shown Haraldr picking off the independent regional kings within Norway, and instituting a new relationship between the king and his richer and more powerful subjects as he extends the range of his power. Within this process, the saga relates both general and specific instances of his antagonising and, ultimately, driving out independently-minded characters, who go and settle in the colonies, particularly in Iceland. At end of Chapter 4, for instance:

> Haraldr konungr var mjǫk gǫrhugall, þá er hann hafði eignazk þau fylki, er nýkomin varu í vald hans, um lenda menn ok ríka búendr ok alla þá, er honum var grunr á, at nǫkkurar uppreistar var af ván. Þá lét hann hvern gera annat hvárt, at gerask hans þjónustumenn eða fara af landi á brott, en at þriðja kosti sæta afarkostum eða láta lífit, en sumir váru hamlaðir at hǫndum eða fótum. Haraldr konungr eignaðisk í hverju fylki óðul ǫll ok allt land, byggt ok óbyggt, ok jafnvel sjóinn ok vǫtnin, ok skyldu allir búendr vera hans leiglendingar, svá þeir, er á mǫrkina ortu, ok saltkarlarnir ok allir veiðimenn, bæði á sjó ok landi, þá váru allir þeir honum lýðskyldir. En af þessi áþján flýðu margir menn af landi á brott, ok byggðusk þá margar auðnar víða, bæði austr í Jamtaland ok Helsingjaland ok Vestrlǫnd, Suðreyjar, Dyflinnar skíði, Írland, Norðmandi á Vallandi, Katanes á Skotlandi, Orkneyjar ok Hjaltland, Færeyjar. Ok í þann tíma fannsk Ísland.

> (Once he had taken possession of those territories that had newly come into his power, King Haraldr was very careful with the landed men, the powerful farmers, and anyone else from whom he suspected any resistance might be foreseen. He made each of them do one of two things: either to become one of his retainers or to leave the country; the third option was to suffer in some way or to be killed — some were maimed in their arms or their legs. King Haraldr took

over all the odal rights in every territory, and all the land both settled and waste, and the sea and the lakes. All the farmers had to be his tenants, and so had those who worked in the woods, the salters, and the hunters by sea and by land: all these became tied to him. But many men fled this subjection by leaving the land; at this time many, scattered empty places were settled, in Jämtland and Hälsingland to the east, and in the west, in the Hebrides and Dublin, Ireland, Normandy in France, Caithness in Scotland, the Orkneys and Shetland and the Faeroes. And at this time Iceland was discovered.)

After the death of Þórólfr Kveld-Úlfsson we have the episode of Ketill Hœngr taking vengeance on the malicious Hildiríðarsynir and fleeing to Iceland. Two chapters later, after Skalla-Grímr's ill-starred attempt to reach a settlement and get compensation from Haraldr, Kveld-Úlfr and Skalla-Grímr follow suit. Into the same basic pattern falls the tale of the elopement and flight of Bjǫrn and Þóra, the parents of Ásgerðr, who becomes Egill's wife.

But Haraldr is not just the figurehead of a new and resented system of vassalage. He is also more than the Machiavellian figure, wielding lonely and inner power, sketched briefly by Gwyn Jones (*loc.cit.*). Haraldr is a figure who can attain truly heroic stature, for instance in the account of the battle of Hafrsfjǫrðr, where a short, quite rapid, steady and accumulative account combines with a well-placed and effectively selected detail of the forward position of Haraldr's own ship to give an image of Haraldr as the leader in a process of high destiny, irresistably forging the kingdom like Virgil's Aeneas or Marvell's Cromwell:

> Haraldr konungr bauð út leiðangri miklum ok dró saman skipaher, stefndi til sín liði víða um land; hann fór ór Þrándheimi ok stefndi suðr í land. Hann hafði þat spurt, at herr mikill var saman dreginn um Agðir ok Rogaland ok Hǫrðaland ok víða til safnat, bæði ofan af landi ok austan ór Vík, ok var þar mart stórmenni saman komit ok ætlar at verja land fyrir Haraldi konungi. Haraldr konungr helt norðan liði sínu; hann

hafði sjálfr skip mikit ok skipat hirð sinni; þar var í stafni Þórólfr Kveld-Úlfsson ok Bárðr hvíti ok synir Berðlu-Kára, Ǫlvir hnúfa ok Eyvindr lambi, en berserkir konungs tólf váru í sǫxum. Fundr þeira var suðr á Rogalandi í Hafrsfirði; var þar in mesta orrosta, er Haraldr konungr hafði átta, ok mikit mannfall í hvárratveggju liði. Lagði konungr framarliga skip sitt, ok var þar strǫngust orrostan; en svá lauk, at Haraldr konungr fekk sigr, en þar fell Þórir haklangr, konungr af Ǫgðum, en Kjǫtvi inn auðgi flýði ok allt lið hans, þat er upp stóð, nema þat, er til handa gekk eptir orrostuna.

(King Haraldr called out a great levy and mustered a fleet. He summoned a troop to himself from far and wide, and left Trondheim for the south. He had learnt that a great army had been assembled in Agder, Rogaland and Hordaland, from distant parts, down from the country and east from the Vík, and that many great men had joined it intending to defend the land against King Haraldr. King Haraldr sailed south with his troop; he himself had a large ship manned by his own retainers. At the prow were Þórólfr Kveld-Úlfsson, Bárðr the White and the sons of Berðlu-Kári, Ǫlvir hnúfa and Eyvindr lambi, and the king's twelve berserks were along the gunwales in the bows. They met in the south at Hafrsfjord in Rogaland. The greatest battle that King Haraldr had ever fought took place there, and there was great loss of life on both sides. The king took his ship to the fore, and there the battle was fiercest; but the result was that King Haraldr gained the victory, and King Þórir haklangr of Agder died, and Kjǫtvi the Rich fled with all of his troop who could still stand, except for those who surrendered after the battle.)

The reader's feeling of satisfaction with Haraldr's success at Hafrsfjǫrðr may be compounded by the fact that here he is fighting in unison with the present 'hero' of the saga, Þórólfr. Even Kveld-Úlfr recognizes the legitimacy of the power of national kings — but not the Norwegian one — when on hearing of Þórólfr's increasingly dangerous situation he advises that he should leave the country and seek service with the king of the English, or of the Danes, or of the Swedes.

Within *Egils saga* Haraldr plays his major role in his relationship with Þórólfr, Egill's uncle. This is a simple tale, of a relationship that changes from friendship into suspicion and jealousy and finally enmity. The seeds of suspicion are sown by the blatantly malicious accusations of the Hildiríðarsynir, the brothers whose claim on the property Þórólfr receives through marriage and the king's gift is disappointed because of their supposedly illegitimate birth. Haraldr's fears of a rival in Þórólfr are soon intensified by Þórólfr's painfully clumsy indiscretions in displaying his wealth and power before the king when the king is his guest, the king, for instance, bringing 300 men to Þórólfr's feast, but Þórólfr 500. Just as nakedly simple as the presentation of the grounds for the loss of friendship is the presentation of the way the king reacts: he is childishly sulky and angry with jealousy at Þórólfr's success:

> Konungr settisk í hásæti; en er alskipat var it efra ok it fremra, þá sásk kongungr um ok roðnaði ok mælti ekki, ok þóttusk menn finna, at hann var reiðr. Veizla var in prúðligsta ok ǫll fǫng in beztu; konungr var heldr ókátr ok var þar þrjár nætr, sem ætlat var.

> (The king sat down on the high seat. But when everyone was in place, both near to him and far from him, the king looked around, turned red and said nothing; people were sure that he was angered. The feast was magnificent and all the provisions were the best; the king was rather sullen, and stayed there three nights, as had been planned.)

And he is absurdly easily swayed by the slander of the Hildiríðarsynir:

> Hildiríðarsynir hǫfðu verit þann vetr með Haraldi konungi ok hǫfðu með sér heimamenn sína ok nábúa. Þeir brœðr váru optliga á tali við konung ok fluttu enn á sǫmu leið mál Þórólfs. Hárekr spurði: "Líkaði yðr vel finnskattrinn, konungr, er Þórólfr sendi yðr?" "Vel,"

sagði konungr. "Þá myndi yðr mart um finnask," sagði
Hárekr, "ef þér hefðið allan þann, sem þér áttuð, en
nú fór þat fjarri; var hitt miklu meiri hlutr, er Þórólfr
dró undir sik. Hann sendi yðr at gjǫf bjórskinn þrjú,
en ek veit víst, at hann hafði eptir þrjá tigu þeira, er
þér áttuð, ok hygg ek, at slíkan mun hafði farit um
annat. Satt mun þat, konungr, ef þú fær sysluna í hǫnd
okkr brœðrum, at meira fé skulu vit fœra þér." En allt
þat, er þeir sǫgðu á hendr Þórólfi, þá báru fǫrunautar
þeira vitni með þeim. Kom þá svá, at konungr var inn
reiðasti.

(The Hildiríðarsynir had been with King Haraldr that
winter, and they had with them their retainers and
neighbours. The brothers were often talking with the
king, and they always accused Þórólfr of the same
thing: "Were you pleased, king, with the Lapps' tribute
that Þórólfr sent you?"
"Indeed," said the king.
"Then you would have been delighted," says Hárekr, "if
you had received everything which belonged to you,
but that was anything but the case. It was much the
larger portion that Þórólfr kept for himself. He sent
you three beaver skins as a gift, but I know for a fact
that he kept back thirty more that belonged to you,
and I believe that it will have been the same with other
wares. The truth is, king, that if you make his authority
over to us brothers we shall bring you more treasure."
And everything that they said against Þórólfr was
supported by the testimony of their companions too.
So it happened, that the king was as angry as he could
be.)

I think, however, we have something more here than
just an infantile character, reflected or created by an
infantile narrative style. If sophistication of any degree is to
be assumed in this section it must surely be in the form of a
sharp stylization of the sequence of events into a stark chain
of cause and effect. Stylization of this kind especially
enhances the feeling of fatedness in the relationship of the
two men, a fate foreseen by Kveld-Úlfr (Ch.5): "vér feðgar
munim ekki bera gæfu til þessa konungs", 'we father and
sons will have no good fortune with this king'.

This conflict between royal family and Kveld-Úlfr's family is fated to pass on to the next generation, Egill's. Drawing upon literary analogues, there are perhaps two fundamental ways in which we might expect to see or interpret the institution of kingship and its relationship to individual characters in terms of fate. On the one hand there is the Shakespearean dictum: "Uneasy lies the head that wears a crown!". In this case an inexperienced Haraldr has multiplied his problems with his power, in particular the problems of facing rival claims for his favour and the readiness of some subjects to manipulate his favour for their personal ends. Such problems in fact would thrive upon the fact of his otherwise being a successful and effective king in terms of enforcing his will through battle. His skill in this respect is particularly clear in his slaying of Þórólfr: it may the wrong thing to do, but he does it in a sure and certain manner.

A different concept of fate is that quoted and explored in the novels of Thomas Hardy: "Character is Fate". Conflict, and the death of Þórólfr, may thus be seen as the determined, fated results of Þórólfr's naivety, which appears in his childlike trust in and longing for a benign, paternal king-figure and his vain love of display and gifts, and of Harald's ambition, to rule all of Norway, and to rule alone. Described thus, in fact, Harald's character is nothing other than an aspect of his being a king, and to this extent there is a degree of overlap or congruency between these two different views of kingship and fate.

This idea of character as fate is strongly supported by the way in which the repetition of the Þórólfr-Haraldr conflict in the next generation is presented. There is an asymetrical balance between the two pairs of Þórólfr-Haraldr and Egill-Eiríkr rather than a parallel. The true parallel to the elder Þórólfr is of course the second Þórólfr, his nephew and Egill's elder brother. As we are told: 'Everyone said that he was going to be most like Þórólfr Kveld-Úlfsson, after whom he was named." (Ch.31). Like his uncle, this Þórólfr is a relatively pliant and trusting character, easy and pleasant in demeanour, and therefore readily agreeable to a king. There is a sense in which this again is the seed of his destruction: it is only Egill, not Þórólfr, who argues against Athelstan's plan that the two should fight separately at Vinheiði. Þórólfr acquiesces: he is lost and Egill survives. The difference in the second generation is that through Skalla-Grímr Egill inherits from his grandfather Kveld-Úlfr an uncompromising, self-sufficient and passionately aggressive character. This character is the opposite of that of the two Þórólfrs.

Egill is the 'hero' of the saga in more than one sense. He is the eponymous hero, the central character after whom the saga is naturally named. He is also heroic in his might and stature, measured incongruously by the extent of the destruction that is the consequence of many of his actions together with the extent of his poetic creativity. He deeply influences many other characters, including the great. Heroic in the classical sense of the word is his defiant independence, an independence which appears particularly significantly in his refusal to move with the times: not temporizing and eagerly indulging in gift-exchanges with the Norwegian kings as his uncle and brother do. This is not to say that Egill's violent self-sufficiency is held up as morally justified, or as desirable or admirable: he is plainly described, like Hrafnkell Freysgoði, as an "ójafnaðarmaðr mikill", 'a greatly unjust man'. He is a fitting saga hero as a man whose life provides an extraordinary spectacle, a marvel: the life of a much-travelled warrior and poet in a period when Scandinavians seem to later generations, to those of early 13th-century Iceland as much as to those of the 20th century, to have achieved scarcely comprehensible feats of conquest and cruel violence.

It asks too much of the reader, then, to view Egill with the uncomplicated sympathy due to the simplest form of literary hero. Similarly Eiríkr, evidently the foil to Egill in the middle section of the saga, the cause of Egill's anger and a threat to him, is in no way an uncomplicated villain. The way in which Eiríkr's involvement moves the plot along is not by his being intrinsically bad or malicious — that character is taken by his queen, Gunnhildr — but rather by his proving himself on crucial occasions to be a relatively weak king. The first conflict between Eiríkr and Egill is by any realistic standards of justice the fault of Egill, the result of his typically psychopathically enraged slaying of Bárðr, whose hospitality towards Egill and his men did not extend to giving them the beer he was keeping for the king. This wretched act (of Egill's) is matched by the rather miserable and feeble vengeance exacted by Gunnhildr, having her brother Eyvindr delude, provoke and stab one of Egill's men, Þorvaldr. Subsequently Eiríkr proves crucially weak at the Gulaþing moot, at which Egill attempts, with justice, to regain his wife's patrimony from Berg-Ǫnundr. As a result of a combination of malice and favouritism, Gunnhildr, through her second brother Álfr Askmaðr, breaks up the court before the case can come to judgement. This results in Egill's first direct attack on Eiríkr, a verbal attack in the form of an indestructible verse lampoon:

> Svá skyldi goð gjalda,
> gram reki bǫnd af lǫndum,
> reið sé rǫgn ok Óðinn,
> rǫn míns féar hónum;
> folkmýgi lát flýja,
> Freyr ok Njǫrðr, af jǫrðum,
> leiðisk lofða stríði
> landǫss, þanns vé grandar.

> (Thus should the gods repay him
> —may the powers and Óðinn be wrath,
> the gods drive the king from the lands —
> for the theft of my goods;
> Freyr and Njǫrðr make the oppressor of people flee
> the lands;
> Landgod be loathsome to the enemy of men,
> the man who destroys the sanctuary.)

The king is cursed because he has failed as a king: he has failed in the kingly role of guarantor or giver of law; and thus he becomes one of those responsible for "rǫn míns féar", 'the theft of my goods'. The failure to preserve the court becomes in the lampoon an act of sacrilege: Eiríkr becomes "þanns vé grandar", 'the man who destroys the sanctuary'.

In the saga this immortal lampoon is soon recompensed with an immortal poem of praise, *Hǫfuðlausn.* By this time the scene has shifted to England. We have seen Egill in England previously, entering into a very different relationship with the English king Athelstan to that which is typical of his relationship with the Norwegian kings. Egill, who otherwise asserts himself as an unshakably conservative champion of the supposed conventions of Viking culture, shows himself respectful to Athelstan to the degree of acquiescence in being "prímsignaðr": undergoing the preliminary baptism which allows him to have familiar dealings with the English christians. It is clear that Athelstan, as Aðalsteinn, the victor at the great battle of Brunanburh or Vinheiði, imposed himself strongly upon the Norse imagination and thus upon subsequent Norse literary traditions. We have preserved in *Egils saga* a fragment of a Norse skaldic panegyric on Athelstan, *Aðalsteinsdrápa:*

> Nú hefr foldgnárr fellda,
> fellr jǫrð und níð Ellu,
> hjalfrsnerrandi, harra
> hǫfuðbaðmr, þría jǫfra;
> Aðalsteinn of vann annat:
> allt's lægra kynfrægjum,
> hér sverjum þess, hyrjar
> hrannbrjótr, konungmanni.

> (Now has the enhancer of battle, towering over the land,
> — land falls under the kinsman of Ella —
> the crown of the tree of kings, felled three kings.
> Athelstan gained something else:
> everything lies lower before the kin-famous king;
> this I swear, breaker of gold.)

— a verse apparently celebrating the English king's victory over an alliance of Norsemen, Britons and Scots at Brunanburh. This verse may or may not have been composed by the same poet as *Hǫfuðlausn, Sonatorrek,*

Arinbjarnarkviða etc. — that is, by Egill — but is far more credibly assignable to the last years of Athelstan's reign than Sigurður Nordal believed (see the footnote to this verse in his *Íslenzk Fornrit* edition, in Chapter 55). That, however, is a side issue. For our purposes it is sufficient that the saga attributes it to Egill and presents it as the product of an affectionate subordinacy, an implicit hero-worship that is utterly different from the hostility of the lampoon of Eiríkr or the ironic reluctance with which *Hǫfuðlausn* is composed.

Athelstan distinguishes himself from Eiríkr as a successful king, a foreign king, and, after a fashion, a king whose legitimacy is more easily recognized in Icelandic literary tradition. His genealogy is traced back to Alfred in Chapter 50 of the saga, although there it is rather unobtrusively noted that Alfred became sole king in England at the same time as Haraldr did in Norway. The titles with which Athelstan is first introduced reveal his importance: he is "inn sigrsæli, fóstri Hákonar ins góða", 'the Victorious, the fosterfather of Hákon the Good". Everything we see of Athelstan is positive and favourable. The cunning he displays before the battle of Brunanburh — like Harald's sure skill in destroying his rivals — is a kingly virtue. He shows a true sense of nobility in his personal payment to Egill in compensation for his dead brother Þórólfr. Certainly he satisfies Egill, a rare feat.

Up to the scene in York, then, we have a comprehensive contrast in both character and attitude towards Eiríkr and Athelstan, to the detriment of Eiríkr. It is, therefore, highly suggestive of the attitudes governing the composition of the saga that it is in exile from Norway, in England, that Eiríkr finally asserts himself and redeems his character to some degree. He is not swayed by Gunnhildr's bloodthirsty egging when facing Egill in either the night or the morning. He acts with rectitude, preserving Egill's life through the night, 'for killings by night are murders'. His speeches throughout both of these scenes are noticeably few and brief, enhancing a sense of dignity that may be found in the way he challenges and then accuses Egill:

Þá litaðisk konungr um, ok sá hann fyrir ofan hǫfuð
mǫnnum, hvar Egill stóð, ok hvessti augun á hann ok
mælti: "Hví vartu svá djarfr, Egill, at þú þorðir at fara á
fund minn? Leystisk þú svá heðan næstum, at þér var
engi ván lífs af mér." Þá gekk Egill at borðinu ok tók
um fót konungi...
    Eiríkr konungr sagði: "Ekki þarf ek at telja upp
sakar á hendr þér, en þó eru þær svá margar ok stórar,
at ein hver má vel endask til, at þú komir aldri heðan
lífs; áttu engis annars af ván, en þú munt hér deyja
skulu; máttir þú þat vita áðr, at þú myndir enga sætt af
mér fá."

(Then the king looked about him, and above the heads
of the men saw where Egill was standing, and narrowed
his eyes upon him and said:
    "Why were you so foolhardy, Egill, as to dare
to come into my presence? You left me in such a
manner last time that you could not expect me to spare
your life."
    Then Egill approached the table and took
hold of the king's foot; [..he recites a verse..]
    King Eiríkr said: "I do not need to list the
charges against you; they are so many and so serious
that any one of them were sufficient reason that you
should never leave here alive. You can expect nothing
but that here you must die. You could have been sure
all along that you would reach no settlement with
me.")

He accepts the poetic ransom offered, *Hǫfuðlausn*, and
permits Egill a safe passage out of his immediate reach. He
shows mercy without capitulating to Egill and Arinbjǫrn,
maintaining that this genuinely noble gesture constitutes no
settlement of the case against Egill:

Eiríkr konungr sat uppréttr, meðan Egill kvað kvæðit,
ok hvessti augun á hann; ok er lokit var drápunni, þá
mælti konungr: "Bezta er kvæðit fram flutt, en nú hefi
ek hugsat, Arinbjǫrn, um mál várt Egils, hvar koma
skal. Þú hefir flutt mál Egils með ákafa miklum, er þú
býðr at etja vandræðum við mik; nú skal þat gera fyrir
þínar sakar, sem þú hefir beðit, at Egill skal fara frá

mínum fundi heill ok ósakaðr. En þú, Egill, hátta svá
ferðum þínum, at síðan, er þú kemr frá mínum fundi
af þessi stofu, þá kom þú aldregi í augsyn mér ok
sonum mínum ok verð aldri fyrir mér né mínu liði. En
ek gef þér nú hǫfuð þitt at sinni; fyrir þá sǫk, er þú
gekkt á mitt vald, þá vil ek eigi gera níðingsverk á þér,
en vita skaltu þat til sanns, at þetta er engi sætt við mik
né sonu mína ok enga frændr vára, þá sem réttar vilja
reka."

(King Eiríkr sat rigid while Egill recited the poem, and
stared piercingly at him. And when the *drápa* was
complete, the king spoke:
        "The poem performed was excellent. And I
have now decided, Arinbjǫrn, what turn my business
with Egill will take. You have pleaded Egill's case with
great commitment when you threaten to fight it out
with me; for your sake it shall be now as you have
asked: Egill shall leave my presence safe and
unmolested. And you, Egill, set your course in such a
way that after you leave my presence in this room you
never come into my sight again, or into my sons' sight,
and never come before me or my troops. And now I
grant you your head for this once. Since you brought
yourself into my power I shall do nothing
dishonourable with you; but you must fully understand
that this constitutes no settlement with me, nor with
my sons, nor with any of our kinsmen who wish to
pursue their rights.")

His firm and controlled behaviour here stands in ironic
contrast to Egill's readiness to temporize to save himself.

The king who displaces Eiríkr from Norway is Hákon.
Hákon the Good is his title in the saga, but he is not a
character the saga shows a very great deal of interest in. He
comes to the fore, and his behaviour in his kingly role
comes in for scrutiny, in the episode of Egill claiming the
property of the savage berserkr he has rather chivalrously
fought and killed, Ljótr. This property, not claimed
immediately by Egill, had been siezed into the king's
possession. Hákon has previously permitted Egill his rights
in the questions of his wife's inheritance, but has warned
Egill subsequently to keep out of Norway. Here he has
acted in a kingly manner where Eiríkr had failed to do so.

In the case of Ljótr's property he refuses Egill's request, which is brought to him by Arinbjǫrn. But a conflict is not allowed to develop: Arinbjǫrn averts a clash by paying Egill compensation for the property himself. Arinbjǫrn subsequently falls into enmity with Hákon by siding with the Eiríkssynir against him, but that is incidental to *Egils saga*. In broad terms Hákon is presented as quite an astute king. He explicitly takes on his family's traditional distrust of Egill's family. He recognizes a threat in Þorsteinn Þóruson, Arinbjǫrn's nephew and Egill's friend, and efficiently and successfully deals with him in the story of the collection of the tribute from the treacherous jarl Arnviðr of Värmland. In general, a few clear strokes delineate Hákon's presence in the saga. Any great deal of attention to him would almost certainly overload the work; there may also be comprehensible reasons for the sagawriter wishing to divert attention from him. His position and attitude towards Egill and Arinbjǫrn seem destined to bring him into disastrous conflict (for one party or the other) with them. He is also a Christian king, bearing a measure of a legitimate right to kingship from Athelstan of England. A conflict of interest looms for the sagawriter, but is avoided.

With the drawing of this literary *cordon sanitaire* around Hákon, the dramatic role of Norwegian kingship as a constant threat, and indeed the relevance of kingship in general as a dramatic issue for Egill's family, is ended. The change is a function of the passage of time: the conflict between the two families, and what they represent, becomes a feature of a past and different age. The tallest stories of hostility and defiance between the two families — that is the least credible and most stylized stories — belong in the most distant past, in the late 9th century when Haraldr Hárfagr is creating a kingdom of Norway and when the independently-minded Viking types are founding a differently structured Icelandic society. Egill, with his nature so clearly inherited from the mysterious half-werewolf Kveld-Úlfr, belongs to a past age: an age in which the ethos of the lonely, uncompromising heroic stance is imagined to have thrived. The conclusion of *Egils saga* must intensify our sense of the passage of time, and of change following the passage of time. Egill is succeeded by his least favourite son Þorsteinn, a son whom he despises for his forbearance that is illustrated in the fundamentally petty quarrel over grazing land provoked by his neighbour Steinarr, and who becomes a Christian. Þorsteinn's patient strategy is shown to succeed with Steinarr, the whole tale ending with Þorsteinn's victory and, remarkably, without either of the principals in the quarrel losing their lives. The heroic age of the Vikings is pictured in the saga as an age that was spectacular and barbaric. The saga also shows this age giving way to one of more civilized, and in literary terms duller, behaviour.

In virtually every medieval European society the king as lawgiver has a crucial role in attempting to uphold such civilized *mores* as these and thus maintaining the good order and security of the community. The stability of society and the right to hold property were like two halves of an arch, held together by its keystone, the king. The direction in which *Egils saga* moves in its great whole implies a craving for the security of a solid structure such as this, and therewith a craving for the presence of the crowned figure who can guarantee it. Egill himself craves a king who will fulfil the royal role properly: first when asking Eiríkr for his rights at the Gulaþing, and subsequently when re-presenting this case to Hákon. It may reasonably be argued that what is at stake for Egill is pride as much as, if not more than, the material value of the property, but his dependence upon the king for satisfaction remains the same. When we look at the deferential and persistent speech made by Egill to Hákon:

> "Ekki máttu, konungr, þegja yfir svá stórum málum, því at allir menn hér í landi, innlenzkir ok útlenzkir, skulu hlýða yðru boði. Ek hefi spurt, at þér setið lǫg hér í landi ok rétt hverjum manni; nú veit ek, at þér munuð mik láta þeim ná, sem aðra menn; þykkjumk ek hafa til þess burði ok frændastyrk hér í landi, at hafa við Atla inn skamma. En um mál okkur Eiríks konungs er yðr þat at segja, at ek var á hans fund, ok skilðumsk vit svá, at hann bað mik í friði fara, hvert er ek vilda. Vil ek bjóða yðr, herra, mína fylgð ok þjónustu; veit ek, at

vera munu hér með yðr þeir menn, er ekki munu
þykkja vígligri á velli at sjá en ek em; er þat mitt
hugboð, at eigi líði langt, áðr fundi ykkra Eiríks
konungs muni saman bera, ef ykkr endisk aldr til; þykki
mér þat undarligt, ef eigi skal þar koma, at þér þykki
Gunnhildr eiga sona uppreist marga."

("King, you cannot be silent concerning such great
matters, for all men here in this country, both natives
and foreigners, must heed your decrees. I have heard
that you enforce law here, and rights for every man.
Now I am sure that you will let me have these like other
men; I believe myself to have birth and a strong
kindred here to match Atli the Short. But on the
subject of my quarrel with King Eiríkr, I can tell you
that I have met with him, and that we parted with him
bidding me go in peace to wherever I would. I want to
offer you, sire, my help and allegiance; I know that
there will be such men with you here who will not
appear more mettlesome than myself on the
battlefield. It is my belief that it will not be long before
you and Eiríkr meet, if both of you should live even so
long. It will be a marvel to me if it does not turn out
that Gunnhildr will seem to you to have raised a mighty
brood of sons.")

'craves' does not seem exaggerated terms to use. There is
an obvious comfort for subjects in finding a strong, benign
and paternal figure in the king, a king to give law, favour,
praise and reward — all of which, despite his family's virtual
feud with the Norwegian royal family, Egill seeks from,
variously, Eiríkr, Athelstan and Hákon.
   It is not an unfamiliar point to make about Egill that
he is a "mass of contrarieties", most obviously because of the
extremes of passion, of friendship and hostility, he can
display. In the question of attitude towards kingship he
appears as a character that is markedly circumscribed by,
and caught in the middle of, a contextual dilemma, a
conflict between a traditional, intuitive mistrust of
Norwegian kingship in Icelandic historical narrative and an
inescapable social need for communal order crowned by a
good and powerful king. This conflict does not, however,
trap and crush *Egils saga* within an unresolved
contradiction. Rather the conflict is mediated by the
timescale, with opposing views of kingship being allowed to

reign at opposite ends of the timescale. Variation in the characters of the kings, for instance in the identifiable inexperience of Haraldr early in his reign and Eiríkr's times of weakness set against Athelstan and Hákon's surefootedness, also helps to balance the opposing forces.

From this point, it would be of value to know if the problem of kingship was a problem consciously faced and solved in this way by the sagawriter, or if *Egils saga* represents a subconscious — perhaps even just a fortuitous — success in blunting the horns of a dilemma. These questions involve the wider issues of the variety of attitudes to kingship met in the records of earlier 13th-century Iceland, and in particular whether the author of the full *Egils saga* that we know was the same as the author of *Heimskringla*, Snorri Sturluson (probably). As is typical of the great sagas, a clear authorial voice is hard to find in *Egils saga*, and it would be rash to hold out hope of quick and definitive answers to any of these wider questions that now arise. Nevertheless we can claim to see the literary character of Egill, in his relations with kings, playing an active role in the efforts of 13th-century Icelanders to express their relationship both with their past and with their present.

Egils saga and other poets' sagas

Alison Finlay
Birkbeck College, University of London

Egils saga is the most distinguished member of a group among the Sagas of Icelanders known as poets' or skalds' sagas. While *Egils saga* is unique in its sustained and deliberate exploration of the temperament of a man of creative genius, there are elements in the portrayal of the hero which are also found in older and shorter examples of the genre, and which probably recall ancient traditional ideas about the nature of the poetic temperament.

It is particularly intriguing that four of these poets' sagas share with each other essentially the same narrative material. They relate the lifelong love of a poet for a woman who becomes the wife of another man. In two sagas, *Bjarnar saga Hítdœlakappa* and *Gunnlaugs saga*, the husband of the beloved woman is himself a poet, and actively cheats the hero of his promised bride. In the other two, *Kormáks saga* and *Hallfreðar saga*, the lover voluntarily relinquishes his chance to marry, but remains to some extent committed to his first love for the rest of his life. With the exception of *Gunnlaugs saga*, these sagas are considered to be among the earliest of the Sagas of Icelanders, predating *Egils saga*. It has been suggested that their common narrative material is to be explained by the direct literary influence of one upon the other, with the theme of unhappy love ultimately borrowed from European versions of the romance of Tristan.[1] I believe, however, that this is too simple an explanation to account for the common characteristics attributed to the poets, which seem inappropriate to the spirit of a tragic love story. These heroes are often presented in an unsympathetic light, sharing traces of the ugliness, aggression and troublesomeness attributed also to Egill. The fact that these elements tend to be rather incompletely assimilated into their sagas — as is not the case in *Egils saga* — suggests that they are vestiges of deep-seated cultural attitudes associated with the art of poetry

and its producers. By comparing the presentation of the
poets in these sagas with that of Egill in *Egils saga*, I shall try
to suggest what some of these attitudes were.

There has long been speculation about the
concentration of erotic themes — supposedly
uncharacteristic of the Sagas of Icelanders — in sagas about
poets. Theodore Andersson writes:

> It is a curious fact that all the skald sagas are partially
> or wholly conceived as love stories. The only skald who
> is not in some way governed by the fair sex is the
> hopeless boor Egill Skallagrímsson. *Gunnlaugs saga,
> Kormáks saga, Bjarnar saga, Hallfreðar saga,* and even
> *Gísla saga* are all constructed on a love conflict. Were
> the skalds more accessible to feminine charms than
> their more prosaic compatriots? Did they make a point
> of immortalizing their amorous contretemps in verse
> while other heroes left their ladies uncelebrated and
> forgotten? The traditions about the Norwegian skalds
> give no indication of erotic preoccupations either
> biographical or poetic. Did the thirteenth century
> simply fancy the skald as a man peculiarly subject to
> the afflictions of love or is there something to the idea
> that this association of love and poetry can be traced to
> the impact of the French troubadour tradition?
> (T. M. Andersson, *The Icelandic Family Saga,*
> 1967, pp. 226-7)

It should be noted that *Egils saga* is not as completely
devoid of romantic interest as Andersson asserts. Not only
do we find in the very first chapter the story of a Norwegian
poet, Qlvir hnúfa, who is involved in an unhappy love affair,
but there is also the hint of such a story associated with Egill
himself. In chapter 42, we are told, without further
explanation, that Egill is too ill to attend the feast
celebrating the wedding of his brother Þórólfr to Ásgerðr,
whom Egill himself later marries after his brother's death.
This suggests an analogue to the incident in *Gunnlaugs saga,*
chapter 11, where the hero declines to attend his rival's
wedding feast. There are versions of the love-triangle story
in *Ívars þáttr* and *Laxdœla saga* in which the rivals are
brothers or cousins. It is significant that Egill's two verses
about his relationship with Ásgerðr (chapter 56) suggest
more emotion than is implied by the prose narrative, in

which his marriage to her seems to be partly a commercial transaction, partly a stage in the process of healing the grief at his brother's death. The first verse contrasts his youthful confident demeanour with his current confusion at the thought of Ásgerðr, which could be a reminiscence of a version of the story in which Egill had been in love with Ásgerðr before her marriage to his brother, but his emotions are not fully revealed. The saga writer seems to have deliberately minimized this aspect of the hero's life.

Even in those poets' sagas where the love story is integral, however, there is less emphasis on emotion than might be expected. A possible explanation of the involvement of poets in love stories might be that the inclusion of verse offered a medium suitable for the expansion of the emotional range beyond that of the customarily restrained style of saga prose. But even in *Kormáks saga*, which includes a large proportion of all the skaldic love poetry that has survived, only thirteen of the 85 verses quoted can be described as amorous. In the poets' sagas as a whole, there is far more verse in which the poets' combative stance is revealed.

An alternative explanation for the prominence of erotic themes in the poets' sagas is that these derive from reminiscences of the poet's role as practitioner of *níð*. This term, which is loosely translated as 'slander', is used in many sagas and legal texts to describe insults of various kinds. It constitutes an attack on a man's honour severe enough to be an offence in law, and the penalties outlined in legal texts can be as heavy as those for killing. The exact reference of the word is not clear, since the legal texts include many instances of punishable insults for which the term *níð* is not used. While some instances are no more than straightforward or maliciously exaggerated comments on events narrated in the saga, there are also some examples in the sagas of what has been referred to as symbolic *níð*.[2] These consist of grotesque fantasies, heavy with hints of sexual perversion and/or animal descent, metaphorically levelling at the victim the dreaded charge of *ergi* — a term covering both homosexuality and cowardice. An example in *Bjarnar saga Hítdœlakappa* is the *Grámagaflím*

— a coarse satirical poem in which the poet describes his enemy's descent from a piece of rotting lump-sucker fish, which made his mother pregnant when she found it on the sea-shore and ate it. *Níð* could also be in pictorial or sculptural form, sometimes accompanied by verse. More obvious sexual symbolism is found in Bjǫrn Hítdœlakappi's depiction of his enemy and himself in a carving, standing one behind the other in postures suggesting a homosexual act:

> Þess er nú við getit, at hlutr sá fannsk í hafnarmarki Þórðar, er þvígit vinveittligra þótti; þat váru karlar tveir, ok hafði annarr hǫtt blán á hǫfði; þeir stóðu lútir, ok horfði annarr eptir ǫðrum. Þat þótti illr fundr, ok mæltu menn, at hvárskis hlutr væri góðr, þeira er þar stóðu, ok enn verri þess, er fyrir stóð. Þá kvað Bjǫrn vísu:
>
>> Standa stœrilundar
>> staðar — — —;
>> glíkr es geira sœkir
>> gunnsterkr at því verki;
>> stendr af stála lundi
>> styrr Þórrøði fyrri.
>
> Þórði þótti ill sú tiltekja ok hneisa, er níð var reist í landi hans, ok hafði þetta á hendr Birni; ok eigi þótti honum yfirbót í vísunni, er Bjǫrn orti, ok reið nú um várit eptir til Bjarnar við sex tigu manna ok stefndi honum til alðingis um níðreising ok vísu.
>
> (*Borgfirðinga sögur*, Íslenzk fornrit III, pp. 154-5).

(It is further related that something appeared on Þórðr's harbour-mark which hardly seemed a token of friendship. It represented two men, one of them with a black hat on his head. They stood stooping, one facing the other's back. It seemed to be an indecent encounter, and people said that the posture of neither of those who stood there was good, and yet that of the one in front was worse. Then Bjǫrn spoke this verse:

> Here are standing helmsmen
> Of harbour landing-places.....;
> suited is the stalwart
> spear-pointer for this action.
> The weapon-wielder's rancour
> weighs on Þórðr foremost.

Þórðr was indignant about this trick, and the disgrace of having this libel set up on his land, and he blamed Bjǫrn for it. He thought that the verse Bjǫrn had composed hardly compensated for it, and so the following spring he rode to Bjǫrn with sixty men and issued a summons to the Alþing against him for putting up the libellous carving and for the verse.)

The saga says that the situation of neither was good, but that that of the man in front (the passive partner) was worse. The rather elliptical expression of this comment, and the omission of two and a half lines from the accompanying verse, hint at the likelihood that many examples of *níð*, as of love poetry, existed in oral circulation but were never recorded, either because of outright indecency or because both had power in law to inflict injury. Although examples of *níð* are found in prose, sometimes in a formulaic cast analogous to verse, it is likely that verbal *níð* was traditionally poetic in form. This supposition is supported by the testimony of the poets' sagas, whose heroes are universally said to be adept in *níð*. The concept no doubt had an ancient pagan origin, though there is little literary evidence for this. One of the most telling pieces of evidence is supplied by the two verses calling on the pagan gods, which are found in chapters 56 and 57 of *Egils saga*, in close proximity to the account of the *níðstǫng* (the pole of slander) which Egill erects against his enemies, Eiríkr and Gunnhildr, in chapter 57:

Hann tók í hǫnd sér heslistǫng ok gekk á bergsnǫs nǫkkura, þá er vissi til lands inn; þá tók hann hrosshǫfuð ok setti upp á stǫngina. Síðan veitti hann formála ok mælti svá: 'Hér set ek upp níðstǫng, ok sný ek þessu' — hann sneri hrosshǫfðinu inn á land, — 'sný ek þessu níði á landvættir þær, er land þetta byggva, svá at allar fari þær villar vega, engi hendi né hitti sitt inni, fyrr en þér reka Eirík konung ok Gunnhildi ór landi.' Síðan skýtr hann stǫnginni niðr í bjargrifu ok lét þar standa; hann sneri ok hǫfðinu inn á land, en hann reist rúnar á stǫnginni, ok segja þær formála þenna allan.

(*Egils saga* skalla-Grímssonar, Íslenzk fornrit II, p.171)

(He took in his hand a hazel pole and climbed on to a
rock that jutted out in the direction of the land. Then
he took a horse's head and thrust it on the pole. Then
he uttered this curse saying, 'Here I erect a Mocking
Pole. And I turn this mockery towards King Eirik and
Queen Gunnhild' — he turned the horse's head in
towards the land — 'I turn this mockery against the
spirits who guard this land so that they may all wander
astray, none reaching nor finding his home until they
drive King Eirik and Queen Gunnhild from the land.'
Then he thrust the pole into a cleft in the rock and let
it stand there. He turned the head towards the land,
and he carved runes on the pole and spoke the full
curse.)

(Translation C. Fell, p.100)

In *Egils saga*, the magical aspect of the practice of *níð*
is emphasized, placing it in the context of other mystical
powers derived from the pagan religion, such as the skilled
use of runes, which the poet has at his command. The
shorter poets' sagas, too, all associate their heroes with *níð*,
but the implications are rather different. Both Hallfreðr
and Gunnlaugr are described as *níðskár* (slanderous), an
unusual word probably used stereotypically of poets, since
there is little in either saga to bear it out. The nicknames of
these poets are also significant. Gunnlaugr's name,
ormstunga (serpent-tongue) speaks for itself; Hallfreðr is
known as *vandræðaskáld* (difficult poet). *Hallfreðar saga*, and
earlier texts which were among its sources, explain the
nickname by reference to the difficulty experienced by King
Óláfr Tryggvason in converting the poet to Christianity —
the other major theme of the saga. The nickname itself,
derived from this well-known story, may have been the
inspiration for the saga writer, or the originator of an
earlier version of the saga, to attach the theme of slander of
a rival in love, already established as a traditional role for a
poet, to one of the most celebrated proponents of skaldic
verse. It is even possible that the nickname referred
originally to the poet's reputation for quarrelsomeness, and
was later transferred to the conversion story, but there is no
evidence for this. In his saga, Hallfreðr recites several

derogatory verses on the subject of the oafish behaviour of his rival, Gríss, when in bed with his wife Kolfinna, and *Landnámabók* includes a probably independent reference to Hallfreðr's *níð*.

Kormákr, too, although he is not described as a slanderous poet, addresses contemptuous verses to his beloved's second husband, and is prosecuted for *níð* after accusing the husband and his brother of cowardice when they fail to appear for a duel.

It is in *Bjarnar saga* that *níð* is both integral to the saga's structure, and symbolically important as an image of the relationships of the rival poets and the woman they quarrel over. The episode of the carved *níð*, referred to above, is significant in that, by representing himself as the active partner in a homosexual act, Bjǫrn is alluding to his actual sexual humiliation of Þórðr by his adultery with Þórðr's wife. So Bjǫrn's *níð* represents both an image of, and an active step in, the process of his revenge on Þórðr for his initial deception in marrying Bjǫrn's betrothed. This act of *níð* is the most offensive in a whole series of insults levelled by the two poets at each other — insults arising out of symmetrical incidents, usually based on homely aspects of everyday life. For instance, Bjǫrn's mockery of Þórðr for being bitten by a seal is answered by Þórðr's attack on Bjǫrn for performing the menial task of picking up a new-born calf from under its mother's tail. The interesting thing about this process is that a whole section of the saga's structure proceeds through the exchange of gradually worsening insults, forming an analogy with the frequent development of saga feud through a series of killings or physical assaults.

It seems clear that skill in *níð* was traditionally associated with poets, and the author of *Egils saga* makes use of this association. But the erotic implications which *níð* has elsewhere were either never present in the sources at his disposal, or were minimized by him as he seems to have minimized romantic elements in other respects. Instead, the magical and religious aspects of *níð* are stressed. In the description of Egill's *níð* there is a much fuller account than elsewhere of the ritual involved in setting up the *níð*-pole, and the two verses of invocation found near this description in the saga call on the gods — Óðinn, Freyr, Njǫrðr and Þórr — for support. The *níðstǫng* is carved with runes, associating it with other incidents in the saga where Egill's skill with runes endows him with supernatural power.

Egill's magical skills can also be seen as an aspect of his affinity with Óðinn. This morally ambivalent, unreliable god was the patron of poets, and in *Sonatorrek* Egill avowedly attributes to Óðinn both his gift of poetry and his passionate temperament. This lament for the death of his beloved son defines the poet's attitude to Óðinn, in that he reproaches the god for turning against him after having bestowed so much upon him. Like other Odinic heroes in the sagas, Egill and those of his forebears from whom he is said to have inherited his looks and temperament are credited with various shape-changing and animal characteristics. In particular their affinities are with the wolf, an animal associated in mythology with Óðinn. Egill's grandfather, Kveld-Úlfr (evening wolf), is said to have acquired his nickname because of his shape-changing propensities. In chapter 65, Egill kills an opponent in a duel by biting through his windpipe — evoking an echo of *Vǫlsunga saga*, where while the Odinic Vǫlsungs are living as werewolves in the forest, Sigmundr bites Sinfjǫtli in the windpipe. Another poet, Víga-Glúmr, is depicted in his saga as a conscious follower of Óðinn, having abandoned his family's traditional allegiance to Freyr, and like Egill he displays aspects of temperament mimicking the unreliability, cunning and moral ambivalence attributed to the god himself.

Odinic affinities are less easy to discern in other poets' sagas. In *Bjarnar saga* and *Hallfreðar saga*, the situation is complicated, to varying degrees, by a Christian element. An important theme in *Hallfreðar saga*, almost obscuring the love story, is the conversion of the poet to Christianity by his patron, the great proselytizing king of Norway, Óláfr Tryggvason. In the course of his conversion the poet recites a series of verses in which he renounces, at first grudgingly and then with increasing fervour, his devotion to the pagan gods. The last of these verses offers an all-embracing rejection of all the major pagan deities: Freyr, Freyja, Njǫrðr and Þórr as well as Óðinn. But the preceding verses speak regretfully of the poet's personal devotion to 'the quick-witted lord of Hliðskjálf', 'for Óðinn's rule well pleased the poet'. This sequence of verses dramatizes the difficulty for a poet, in particular, of abandoning the religion so closely bound up with his own art.

Bjǫrn Hítdœlakappi is represented as an equally devoted follower of the other great Christian king, St. Óláfr, and the saga reveals a hagiographic strain disconcerting alongside the crudity of the *nið*-verses and their setting in the workaday domestic environment. Bjǫrn is said to have composed a *drápa* in honour of St. Thomas the Apostle, and to have built a church at his home at Vellir. When he is buried he is wearing a garter which had belonged to St. Óláfr, and when his body is later disinterred the leg wearing the garter is found to be uncorrupted — a motif familiar from saints' lives. There is no attempt to reconcile this element of piety with the contrasting emphasis, particularly strong in this saga, on the poet as practitioner of *nið*. There is no question of representing Bjǫrn as a follower of Óðinn in other than the most conventional sense: his verse, like that of most skalds, includes some formal declarations such as 'I work to produce Óðinn's beer' (v.32), or, combining the roles of poet and warrior, 'Óðinn will again bring the man wise in metres into battle' (v.30). One of his verses, though, reveals a strange blend of Christian and pagan symbolism (v.34). He describes his dream of a helmet-wearing woman inviting him home — that is, to his death. The helmet and the summons to the other world suggest the valkyrie, Óðinn's handmaiden; but she is described as 'the helmet-covered red Ilmr of arm-serpents [woman] of the prince of day's fire': an explicit reference to the Christian God.

As with Egill, a certain amount of animal imagery is associated with Bjǫrn. He too kills an armed man without using a weapon, though he strangles him rather than using his teeth. In his heroic last defence, where again he fights almost unarmed, one of his enemies employs animal imagery evoked by the hero's name: 'I believe that now I shall hunt the bear which we all want to hunt' .

But unlike *Egils saga*, *Bjarnar saga* makes little specific use of this probably traditional characteristic. Bjǫrn's animalistic qualities simply offer vague support for his warlike skills; Egill's wolfish propensities align him with the pagan sphere of Óðinn. Neither Gunnlaugr nor Kormákr is associated with Óðinn in any way in their respective sagas, though the fragments of Kormákr's verse which survive outside the saga have a pagan (though not specifically Odinic) orientation.

In appearance, Egill is by far the most striking, not to say intimidating, of the poets. It has loosely been suggested that poets were traditionally presented as dark and ugly,[3] but a glance at the descriptions of the heroes I am discussing shows the inaccuracy of this.

Bjǫrn Hítdœlakappi is described as 'snimma mikill vexti ok rammr at afli, karlmannligr ok sœmiligr at sjá .. inn skǫruligsti maðr ok vel menntr' (Íslenzk fornrit III, pp.112-3) (tall at an early age, with a powerful physique, masculine and handsome to look at .. a most impressive man, and well-bred), and at a later point in the saga, 'Bjǫrn var mikill maðr vexti ok vænn ok freknóttr, rauðskeggjaðr, skrúfhárr ok dapreygðr ok manna bezt vígr' (p.197) (Bjǫrn was a man of great stature, handsome and freckled, red-bearded and curly-haired, weak-sighted, but an excellent fighting man). Kormákr is said to be 'svartr á hár ok sveipr í hárinu, hǫrundljóss ok nǫkkut líkr móður sinni, mikill ok sterkr, áhlaupamaðr í skapi' (Íslenzk fornrit VIII, p.206) (with black curly hair and a bright complexion, rather like his mother, tall and strong, and impetuous in temperament).

The descriptions of Hallfreðr and Gunnlaugr are so similar that it seems likely that the later *Gunnlaugs saga* has borrowed from *Hallfreðar saga*, in which the hero is described as follows:

Hann var snimma mikill ok sterkr, karlmannligr ok
skolbrúnn nǫkkut ok heldr nefljótr, jarpr á hár, ok fór
vel; skáld var hann gott ok heldr níðskár ok
margbreytinn; ekki var hann vinsæll.
(Íslenzk fornrit VIII, p.141)

(He was tall and strong at an early age, manly and with
heavy brows (?), with a rather ugly nose and chestnut
hair which suited him well; he was a good poet, rather
slanderous, and erratic; he was not popular).

Compare the description of the hero of *Gunnlaugs
saga*:

Svá er sagt frá Gunnlaugi, at hann var snimmendis
bráðgǫrr, mikill ok sterkr, ljósjarpr á hár, ok fór allvel,
svarteygr ok nǫkkut nefljótr ok skapfelligr í andliti,
miðmjór ok herðimikill, kominn á sik manna bezt,
hávaðamaðr mikill í ǫllu skaplyndi ok framgjarn
snimmendis ok við allt óvæginn ok harðr ok skáld mikit
ok heldr níðskár ok kallaðr Gunnlaugr ormstunga.
(Íslenzk fornrit III, p.59)

(It is said of Gunnlaugr that he was mature at an early
age, tall and strong, with light chestnut hair which
suited him well, with black eyes and a rather ugly nose,
and a well-shaped face; slender in the waist and broad-
shouldered; a most accomplished man, very haughty in
all aspects of his disposition, energetic from an early
age and headstrong and harsh besides; a great poet
and rather slanderous. He was called Gunnlaugr
Serpent-Tongue.)

The suggestion that all poets are said to be dark and
ugly has probably arisen under the influence of the
particularly striking description of the hero of *Egils saga*:

Egill var mikilleitr, ennibreiðr, brúnamikill, nefit ekki
langt, en ákafliga digrt, granstœðit vítt ok langt, hakan
breið furðuliga, ok svá allt um kjálkana, hálsdigr ok
herðimikill, svá at þat bar frá því, sem aðrir menn váru,
harðleitr ok grimmligr, þá er hann var reiðr; hann var
vel í vexti ok hverjum manni hæri, úlfgrátt hárit ok
þykkt ok varð snimma skǫllóttr; en er hann sat, sem
fyrr var ritat, þá hleypði hann annarri brúninni ofan á

kinninna, en annarri upp í hárrœtr; Egill var svarteygr
ok skolbrúnn.

(Íslenzk fornrit II, p. 143)

(Egil's features were strongly marked; a broad
forehead, heavy brows, a nose not long but very wide,
lips broad and full, the chin unusually broad and the
whole jawline, a thick neck and shoulders broader than
most men have, harsh-looking and fierce when he was
angry. He was of good size, taller than anyone else,
with thick wolfgrey hair, and he soon became bald.
While he sat, as was said above, he drooped one
eyebrow down towards his cheek, raising the other up
to the roots of his hair. Egil had black eyes and dark
brows).

(Translation C. Fell, p.84)

Of the other poets only Kormákr can be characterized
as dark, and even he refers in one of his verses to his 'alfǫlr'
(very pale) complexion. What the descriptions of the poets
do have in common, however, is the suggestion of unusual,
striking and strongly-marked appearance. Egill, Gunnlaugr
and Hallfreðr all have ugly noses; both Egill and Hallfreðr
are said to be 'skolbrúnn', an obscure word, possibly
suggesting either heavy or mobile eyebrows. It is interesting
to note the inconsistency in the shorter poets' sagas
between the abrasive qualities which tend to be associated
with poets, and the stereotypical approving terms applied
equally conventionally to a saga hero. For instance, the
description of Gunnlaugr is very similar to that of Hallfreðr
and may have been modelled on it, but it has been
modified by the addition of features that make the hero
more obviously attractive: he has a well-shaped face, broad
shoulders, and a slender waist. I would suggest that it is
particularly in this comparatively late saga that
preoccupations that we would consider appropriate to a
love-story have been superimposed on an older, harsher
idea of a poet as a rather dangerously eccentric outsider.

In temperament, we are told, the poets tend to be
erratic and unstable, perhaps on the model of that master
of unpredictability, Óðinn. Again, in the shorter sagas, this
is asserted as if by convention without support from the
narrative. Hallfreðr, for instance, is said to be

'margbreytinn' (changeable), but there is no clear illustration of this trait in the saga. On the other hand, there is ample justification for the description of Kormákr as an 'áhlaupamaðr' (impetuous man) — the prime example being his failure to come to his own wedding. Gunnlaugr, too, is criticized in his saga for being 'óráðinn' (unsettled), and it is significant that the occasion for this is his attempt to divide his attention between his betrothal and his ambition to travel abroad.

Egils saga goes far beyond such brief suggestions by dramatizing the hero's temperamental extremes. He is prone to violent fits of aggression and cruelty, and, on the other hand, attacks of moodiness and depression; he is avaricious, a vice never mentioned in the other poets' sagas, and suspicious and hostile even to those closest to him. In its full-blown characterization of the poet's temperament, the saga has, on the one hand, emphasized and given life to attributes hinted at in the briefer compass of the shorter poets' sagas: unpredictability, supernatural insight, recklessness and unpopularity. On the other hand, it adds more individualistic details, some of which may indeed derive from European sources, though of a learned rather than a romantic kind.

It has been suggested that the poets' sagas, and in particular *Egils saga*, have been influenced by twelfth-century versions of the Aristotelian theory of the link between the frenzy of artistic creation and the temperamental state of melancholy.[4] It is theoretically possible that saga writers early in the thirteenth century could have been influenced by learned theories of the humours and their influence on temperament. Any such influence, however, must have fallen on ground well conditioned to receive it by the habits of psychological analysis already developed in the native tradition of saga composition.

The characteristics conventionally attributed to the melancholy temperament underwent many changes of substance and emphasis throughout antiquity and the medieval period. Indeed, contradictions were inherent even in the earliest stages, as is shown by the paradoxical definition, in the pseudo-Aristotelian Problem XXX.I, of melancholy as both a debilitating mental and physical disorder and, at the same time, the prerequisite for inspiration in exceptional men: 'philosophers, statesmen, poets and artists'. The author of the Problem conceives of the melancholy temperament as governed not by particular characteristics, but rather by a tendency to violent extremes of somewhat contradictory states:

> Now if black bile, being cold by nature and not superficially so, is in the stated condition, it can induce paralysis or torpor or depression or anxiety when it prevails in the body; but if it is overheated it produces cheerfulness, bursting into song, and ecstasies and the eruption of sores and the like...Among those who constitutionally possess this temperament there is straight away the greatest variety of characters, each according to his individual mixture. For example, those who possess much cold black bile become dull and stupid, whereas those who possess much hot bile are elated and brilliant or erotic or easily moved to anger and desire, while some become more loquacious. Many too are subject to fits of exaltation and ecstasy .. and this is how Sibyls and soothsayers arise and all that are divinely inspired...Such a constitution also makes for great differences in behaviour in dangerous situations in that many of these people react inconsistently in frightening circumstances; for according to the condition of their bodies at a given time in relation to their temperament, they behave now one way now another: the melancholy temperament, just as it produces illnesses with a variety of symptoms, is itself variable.
>
> (*Saturn and Melancholy*, pp. 23-5)

The dangerously stimulating effects of melancholy are likened to those of wine, and melancholy people are generally stimulated to lust: 'wine excites sexual desire, and Dionysus and Aphrodite are rightly said to belong together, and most melancholy persons are lustful. For the sexual act is connected with the generation of air.'

In *Egils saga*, the exploration of the poet's consciousness and temperament is more deliberately developed than in the shorter poets' sagas, and the saturnine aspect more consistently emphasized. It may be that a later, more learned author developed the beliefs underlying the earliest poets' sagas in the light of the classical theory, which shows some remarkable consonances with Icelandic tradition. For example, the baldness of Egill and his father, and the lycanthropy of his grandfather, both of which could be identified as classic symptoms of melancholy, were clearly not added by the saga author, since they are enshrined in the names Skalla-Grímr and Kveld-Úlfr. Features which can be established as characteristic of adherents of Óðinn can be assumed to derive from the traditional association of that god with poetry. However, the greater emphasis in *Egils saga* on features appropriate to the melancholy temperament, and the author's concern to delineate in detail the mind of a man of genius, suggest that the saga writer may well have consciously emphasized those aspects of tradition which accorded with some learned description of the melancholy temperament known to him.

It is significant that *Egils saga* is only marginally concerned with love. The Icelandic association of poets with love cannot owe anything to the learned tradition, since the association is most prominent in those sagas which do not examine the hero's temperament in depth. However, the fact that 'Aristotle' independently made the association between artistic creativity and erotic tendencies supports the view of the erotic element as the natural counterpart of the depiction of the poet as a man of great imaginative capacities.

It is incontrovertible that several poets share features both of appearance and personality that seem to owe nothing to the European romance tradition. The typical romance hero, Tristan, is generally presented as a paragon of virtues and accomplishments, as he is in the Norwegian *Tristrams saga ok Ísondar*, translated from the Anglo-Norman Tristan of Thomas:

> He was extremely quick to learn, and was instructed in this science, and became fluent in all kinds of languages; next he learned to play the harp, so that there was no one more skilled or famous for it; no one was his equal for good-nature, generosity and courtly behaviour, for wisdom and good counsel and courage.

No one could match him for politeness and
seemliness, so much did his attainments increase.

The heroes of the poets' sagas, on the other hand, are
often described as ugly and individualistic, unsociable and
dangerous, their main accomplishment the art of verse-
making in its most threatening aspect. These attributes are
perceptible even where, as in *Bjarnar saga* and *Gunnlaugs
saga*, some attempt is made to mellow the hero's character.
However, the saturnine strain is not presented consistently
enough (as it is in *Egils saga*) to support the supposition that
it is influenced to any extent by learned lore about the
humours.

The involvement of poets in stories about love, and in
particular about love as a source of conflict, is most likely to
derive from neither of these sources, but from the
traditional role of the poet as practitioner of *níð*, the satire
which in its most fundamental and powerful form relied on
erotic symbolism. In *Bjarnar saga*, *Kormáks saga* and
Hallfreðar saga, *níð* is actively used in the conflict between
rivals in love, though only in *Bjarnar saga* does the
accusation form a symbolic reflection of the actual conflict.
If it can be accepted that the influence of the Provençal
troubadours did find its way into the shaping of these sagas,
the strong satirical element in much of their verse may have
reinforced the tradition.

---

1   Bjarni Einarsson, *Skáldasögur*, Reykjavík, 1967 (In
Icelandic, with English summary).
2   See Folke Ström, *Níð, ergi and Old Norse moral attitudes*,
The Dorothea Coke Memorial Lecture, 1973, and Preben
Meulengracht Sørensen, *The Unmanly Man. Concepts of
Sexual Defamation in Early Northern Society* (translated by Joan
Turville-Petre) Odense, 1983.
3   Margaret Clunies Ross, "The Art of Poetry and the
Figure of the poet in *Egils saga*", *Parergon* 22 (1978) 3-12.
4   Margaret Clunies Ross, *op. cit.* For an account of
classical and medieval beliefs about melancholy, see R.
Klibansky, E. Panofsky and F. Saxl, *Saturn and Melancholy*,
London, 1964.

Egill's longer poems:
Arinbjarnarkviða and *Sonatorrek*

Carolyne Larrington
St. John's College, Oxford.

Gabriel Turville-Petre called Egill Skalla-Grímsson 'the greatest of all the scalds' (*Origins of Icelandic Literature* p.40); despite recent re-evaluations of the work of Norwegian court poets, Egill's position remains unchallenged. Although Sigurður Nordal stigmatized *Hǫfuðlausn* as 'efnilitið, og minna listaverk en bezti skáldskapur Egils annar' (slight in content, and a lesser work of art than the best of Egill's other poetry), it is this poem which seems to have been the focus of critical attention. No doubt the dramatic circumstances of its composition and performance, and its innovative metre, have captured scholars' imaginations. Although Sigurður does not specify which poems are Egill's 'bezti skáldskapur annar', it is the aim of this essay to show that, while *Sonatorrek* is the most likely candidate, the underestimated *Arinbjarnarkviða* deserves to stand beside the elegy in poetic skill. The two poems, 'noble ruins' though they may be, tower over the *lausavísur* as twin monuments to Egill's poetic career.

Similarities of theme and vocabulary suggest that all three long poems were composed by the same poet; if *Hǫfuðlausn* can be plausibly dated to the tenth century, then we may, at least for the purposes of this essay, assume that the historical Egill Skalla-Grímsson, rather than the saga author, (Snorri?), or an unknown third person, is the author of the poems under discussion.

Both *Sonatorrek* and *Arinbjarnarkviða* have problematic relationships to the manuscripts of the saga: moreover they are imperfectly preserved. Manuscript M (Möðruvallabók) gives only the first verse of *Sonatorrek*, while the more recent Ketilsbók (K) gives the whole poem. As far as *Arinbjarnarkviða* is concerned, K has no text; M has a lacuna after one verse, but the poem is written out, in a different hand, at the end of the saga. The final verses are near illegible, and the text printed in ÍF has been completed from the *Snorra Edda* and the *Málskrúðsfræði* of Óláfr *hvítaskald*, our sole authority for the last two verses. Both poems are placed in the long Chapter 78 of the saga, and in both cases the poem fits rather uneasily into its prose context. Although the genesis of *Sonatorrek* is described in detail, (the bereaved father threatening to starve himself to death until persuaded to compose an *erfidrápa* (memorial poem) by his daughter, Þorgerðr), the author has to insert a hasty parenthesis to account for the reference to Gunnarr, the second dead son 'sá ok andazk litlu áðr' (he had also died a little previously). Gunnarr's existence is recorded in Ch. 66, but nothing else has been told of him. The parenthesis is vital if the poem is to be understood, but the pace of the whole episode, which should culminate in Egill's triumphant rescue of himself in the face of death and despair, is dissipated by the aside.

Arinbjarnarkviða is composed when Egill hears the good news that Arinbjǫrn has returned to Norway with Haraldr *gráfeldr*, his foster-son, and is at last enjoying a position of high esteem in the kingdom, ruling over Fjarðafylki. Ms. K tells us that Egill dispatched the poem to Norway (though, frustratingly, not how the text was conveyed), an observation which fits the prose context and would clarify the references to a listening audience in the poem. Yet Arinbjǫrn's death, fighting alongside Haraldr *gráfeldr*, is announced only a few lines after the completion of *Arinbjarnarkviða*, news to which Egill responds with a rather conventional *lausavísa*, lamenting the loss of generous patrons — 'Where shall I seek generous men to give me silver for my poetry now?' he asks. At times, *Arinbjarnarkviða* sounds very much like the kind of memorial lay that we find in *Glymdrápa*, a praise-poem celebrating the achievements of the dead lord. It is only the saga context, and a small number of present tense verb forms (among a majority of preterite forms) in the text which suggest that Arinbjǫrn is still alive at the time of composition.

Arinbjarnarkviða opens with the poet's attention firmly focussed on himself, 'emk hraðkvæðr' (I am swift of speech) 1^1, commenting on the act of making poetry, a preoccupation shared with *Hǫfuðlausn* and *Sonatorrek*, as he invites his audience to admire his fluency, put to work for a public and socially approved end. The general themes of the poem are addressed already in the first two verses: the nature of nobility, later exemplified by Arinbjǫrn, consisting in generosity, 'mildinga' (generous lords) 2^6, and courage, 'jǫfurs dáðum' (a lord's great deeds) 1^6; and their opposites: 'gløggvinga' (misers) 1^4, and 'skrǫkberǫndum' (lying boasters) 2^2. Egill veers away from a predictable elaboration of his theme, however, turning abruptly to his own memory of the climactic encounter with Eiríkr *blóðøx* in York. His opponent is powerful, 'ríks konungs' 3^3, stubborn, 'við stirðan hug' 4^6, and terrifying to an almost supernatural degree:

Vasaat tunglskin	That moonlight was not	
tryggt at líta	safe to gaze at	
né ógnlaust	nor without dread	
Eiríks bráa,	from Eiríkr's brows,	
þás ormfránn	when serpent-glittering	
ennimáni	a forehead-moon	
skein allvalds	hone with a ruler's	
ægigeislum.	terror-beams.	5

The serpent metaphor, combining with 'ægigeislum', and 'ýgs hjálmi' (helm of dread) 4^2, recalls the mysterious 'œgishjálmr' (helm of terror) which the dragon Fáfnir was said to possess, which gave him (an ultimately illusory) power over all living things. Although Eiríkr's majesty is unnaturally awe-inspiring, Egill does not quail: rather he stresses his own audacity, 'drók djarfhǫtt' (I drew on a hood of daring) 3^5; 'bera þorðak' (I dared to bring) 6^2. The two opponents are well matched.

Egill harnesses the myth of the mead of poetry, itself a tale of danger in a strange hall, to provide an apposite kenning for the poem he performed: 'bólstrverð ... maka hæings markar' (the pillow-price of the mate of the forest's

fish) 6^{1-4}. The 'forest's fish' is the snake, the form which
Óðinn took when he bored through the rock to claim the
mead of poetry according to *Hávamál* 106 and the *Snorra
Edda;* the mate is then Gunnlǫð, with whom he slept to gain
the mead, the 'bólstrverð'.

The two situations are analogous. Óðinn knew himself
to be in mortal danger as he schemed to get the mead: 'svá
hætta ek hǫfði til' (thus I risked my head), he recalls in
Hávamál 106^6. Óðinn's tone is light-hearted, looking back
exultantly on a successful exploit. In *Arinbjarnarkviða* too,
Egill jokes about the apparent worthlessness of the reward
— though 'golli betri' (better than gold) 9^6 to him — for
his poetry: 'ulfgrátt ... hattar staup ... tvau ... sǫkk sámleitt'
(wolf-grey 7^5 ... a lump for a hood 7^7 ... two ... dark-
coloured gems 8^{2-3}). The comedy conceals the real danger
of death and decapitation, hinted at by the nightmarish
glimpses of the listening audience in Eiríkr's hall as a
collection of dismembered body parts: 'hvers manns /
hlusta munnum ... fyrir hilmis kné ... tannfjǫlð með tungu
þák / ok hlertjǫld' (every man's ears' mouths 6^{7-8} ... before
the prince's knee 8^8 ... a multitude of teeth I received with
my tongue and listening-tents) 9^{1-3}. There is no doubt as to
the seriousness of the stakes.

With v. 10, the focus of the poem moves from the
double vision of the poet performing to his audience, now
in Iceland, then in York, to the figure at his side: 'tryggr vinr
minn / sás trúa knáttak' (my loyal friend / the one whom I
could trust) 10^{5-6} Egill states simply. The near-repetition of
'tryggr', 'trúa' recalls those stanzas of *Hávamál* defining the
friend in just such basic terms: 'veiztu, ef þú vin átt, þann er
þú vel trúir ...' (know, if you have a friend, one whom you
really trust ... 44^{1-2}; cf. also 119^{5-6}). The revelation of the
friend's identity is teasingly delayed until v. 11, where the
name is triumphantly and ringingly declaimed in the first
line. Although he is Egill's friend, Arinbjǫrn is also the 'vinr
þjóðans, es vættki ló' (friend of the prince, who never lied)
11^{5-6}. The conflict of loyalties which Arinbjǫrn experiences
is allusively evoked, but the depth of the poet's trust in his

friend does not permit any shadow of suspense to fall over the poem. We know that Arinbjǫrn will stand by Egill.

Verse 12 is too damaged to allow interpretation, but in v. 13 Egill returns to his first theme — what is he doing by making this poem? The contrasts of vv. 1 and 2 are restated as the contrast between good friend, Arinbjǫrn, and the hypothetical bad friend 'vinþjófr ... váljúgr ... heitrofi' (thief of friendship ... great liar... tearer of promises) 13[1,3,6] that Egill would become if he failed to recompense Arinbjǫrn for his friendship. Ideas of exchange and reward — praise for friendship, blame for stinginess, heads for poetry — form the structural underpinning of *Arinbjarnarkviða*. Egill drives a good bargain here, a bargain concluded in friendship and fairness rewarding Arinbjǫrn for his loyalty, in contrast with the apparently bad bargain which Egill has made in his contract with Óðinn, a bargain examined closely in *Sonatorrek*.

Two different conceits are now employed to express the hard work involved in making a poem; unlike *Sonatorrek* where the emphasis on difficulty reveals Egill's own inner despair, here the labour which poetry-making demands adds value to the gift which Egill offers his friend. In v.14 the conceit is of the steep path, 'bratt stiginn' 14[3], which must be climbed by the feet of verse, 'bragar fótum' 14[4], an image satisfyingly completed in the poem's final verse where Egill claims:

hlóðk lofkǫst	I piled up a cairn of praise
þanns lengi stendr	which will stand for a long time
óbrotgjarn	not keen to break
í bragar túni.	in the meadow of poetry. 25[5-8]

The unusual image recalls Horace's boast in *Odes*, iii, 30: 'Exegi monumentum aere perennius / regalique situ pyramidum altius' (I have built a monument more durable than bronze / and loftier than the royal setting-up of pyramids), although, if *Arinbjarnarkviða* is genuinely Egill's, his image must of course be independent in origin. More typical of Egill's visioning of his own work is the conceit of v.15, where the subject-matter (*efni*), Arinbjǫrn's praise, is so much raw timber, easily worked by Egill 'auðskæf ómunlokri' (easy to smooth with the voice-plane) 15[1-2]. As we shall see, metaphors drawn from timber and woodworking reappear in *Sonatorrek*.

The name so proudly produced in v. 11 is playfully and riddlingly hidden in 16[7-8]: 'bjóða bjǫrn birkis ótta'. The birch's terror, 'birkis ótta', is fire; the edge, 'bjóða', of fire is the hearth, 'arin'; the bear, 'bjǫrn', of the hearth is Arinbjǫrn. The verses which follow pile up epithets of generosity and graciousness as typical of Arinbjǫrn's way of life, celebrating his magnanimity, 'mildgeðr' 16[5]; his popularity, 'vinreið af vegum ǫllum' (the ride of friends from all directions) 18[5-6], and his ability to get on with all sorts of people, a difficult task, the misanthropic poet observes: 'kveðka ... auðskeft almanna spjǫr' (I do not say that it is easy to shaft the spear of most people), a gnomic idiom again illuminated by *Hávamál* (v.126).

Verse 22 seems to be a transitional verse; although the subject is still Arinbjǫrn's generosity, the metaphors are violent: 'fégrimmr ... dolgr Draupnis niðja ... hringum hættr / hoddvegandi' (fierce to money 22[1] ... enemy of the descendants of Draupnir (Óðinn's ring which drops eight of equal weight every ninth night) 22[3-4] ... dangerous to rings / hoard-smiter 22[7-8]). The warlike images look forward to the partially-preserved v. 23 which introduces Arinbjǫrn's life-story 'fjǫlsáinn með friðar spjǫllum' (much sown with destructions of peace) 23[3-4], suggesting that the missing verses might have balanced the sequence 16-22, which demonstrates Arinbjǫrn's open-handedness, with a similar series celebrating his courage in battle.

As the poem stands, however, the curious v. 24 has no link with what precedes it. The verse appears to comment on Arinbjǫrn's current fortunes at a much lower ebb than the saga prose suggests, while the references to the sea, 'þat's órétt / ef orpit hefr / á máskeið / mǫrgu gagni' (That is not right if he has cast away his many advantages on the sea-mew's path) 24[1-4], seem to fit better with the account of

Arinbjǫrn's death, fighting in the sea-battle of Limfjǫrðr alongside Haraldr *gráfeldr.* Arinbjǫrn stands, and perhaps falls, by his prince, just as, long ago in York, he stood by Egill. 'þvís veitti mér' (for he supported me), 24[8], is Egill's final tribute — perhaps epitaph? — to his friend. The concluding verse, looking back to the path of poetry clambered up in 14[3-4], re-asserts Egill's pride in his achievement, and brings us back from York, from the great halls of Norway and the seascape of v. 23 to the Icelandic farm and the farmer-poet at his 'morginverkum' (morning-work) 25[4], making a memorial-cairn for his friend.

Appreciation of *Arinbjarnarkviða* comes only with a sense of the full weight of the saga and Egill's personal history (which may be why the poem has seldom been anthologised). We need to bear in mind the long friendship of Egill and Arinbjǫrn, a friendship contracted at first sight between the powerful lord's son and the difficult younger brother of the accomplished and sociable Þórólfr. Over the years Arinbjǫrn has been host to Egill, fought alongside him, and, on numerous occasions, mediated on Egill's behalf with a succession of rulers. The confrontation between Egill, Eiríkr and Arinbjǫrn in York is taken in *Arinbjarnarkviða* as a single occasion which stands for all; not only is it pre-eminent in drama, and in the stakes for which both Egill and Arinbjǫrn gamble, it is the one moment where Arinbjǫrn, the diplomat and politician, is forced to choose publicly between the lord he has followed faithfully into exile in England and his old friend. Arinbjǫrn chooses Egill of course, and Egill's recollection of his friend, standing 'á hlið aðra' (at my side) 10[4] is much more than a record of spatial dispositions at the climactic moment: it recognizes the daring of Arinbjǫrn's gamble on Eiríkr's acceptance of the demands of kingly magnanimity.

Arinbjǫrn has done much for Egill then, but we should be wary of seeing the favours as flowing only in one direction. Egill has undertaken a dangerous mission to Vermaland in the stead of Arinbjǫrn's nephew, Þorsteinn — a mission imposed by the hostile Hákon *Aðalsteinsfóstri* who

is persecuting Arinbjǫrn's family for his allegiance to the
Eiríkssynir. The final chapters of *Egils saga* are, as de Vries
points out, a badly-unified construction pieced together
from the stories recounting the origins of the two great
poems and a number of anecdotes from Egil's old age.
According to the saga's internal chronology, Egill would
have been around fifty when he composed these two poems,
and had a good thirty years of life ahead. Thus we must not
be misled by the saga's portrait of Egill in old age as a
grasping miser into believing that this character trait
controls his relationship with Arinbjǫrn also. Far more
important is Egill's sense of justice, monitoring and finely
adjusting the exchange of favours and gifts which, as
Hávamál tells us, is the method by which friendship is
maintained. *Arinbjarnarkviða* stands as a magnificent
acknowledgement of a lifetime's friendship, demonstrating
Egill's understanding of the social and public function of
poetry, contrasting with the personal and psychological
ends to which poetic activity is painfully directed in
Sonatorrek.

The problems of interpretation which
Arinbjarnarkviða offers are caused by the poem's damaged
state; the language itself is straightforward, with a simple
assurance consonant with Egill's claims for fluency and ease
in the first verse. Not so *Sonatorrek*. Despite the omissions
and lacunae, the poem's design remains reasonably clear; it
is in the poetic language that difficulties abound, in the
interpretation of kennings and individual words. The
audience is forced to match the effort which Egill himself
tells us was needed to haul up the material of poetry from
the depths of his heart, 'né hógdrœgt / ór hugar fylgsni'
(nor is it easy to draw [verse] from the hiding-place of
thought). Space does not permit full commentary on
textual problems here; I refer the reader to Nordal's
edition, and Turville-Petre's translation and commentary in
Scaldic Poetry.

In contrast then with *Arinbjarnarkviða*, composed with
ease from a generous spirit ('mildgeðr', *Abkv.* 16[5]),
Sonatorrek begins in laboriousness, despairing that the poetic

enterprise can be achieved: 'esa nú vænligt / of Viðurs þýfi' (it is not now to be hoped for the theft of Óðinn) 1^{5-6}. Allusions to the myth of the stealing of the poetic mead, the 'fagnafundr ... ár borinn / ór Jǫtunheimum' (joyful find ... brought long ago from the world of the giants) $2^{5,7-8}$, emphasise the difficulty of that venture also. Though 'fagnafundr' contrasts with Egill's despairing mood in the first verses, it may look forward to the end of the poem, where resolution — or at least a lessening of Egill's grief — will be achieved through recognition of the value of the poetic gift which Óðinn has bestowed on his poet.

Verse 3 is obscure; Nordal and Turville-Petre interpret it as further development of the allusion to the myth of the poetic mead, although the references to boathouses and ships may hint at the immediate cause of Egill's grief, the drowning of his son Bǫðvarr. Thus the verse would look ahead to v. 4 which opens with 'þvít' (thus). The frequent hypotactical constructions in the poem's syntax — the use of 'þótt' (though), 'ef' (if), and 'þvít' (since), cited by M. C. van den Toorn as evidence of 'kausal-logisch' (causal-logical) reasoning in Egill's argument with himself — show that *Sonatorrek* is by no means an unthinking and purely emotional wail of despair. The catharsis which Egill finds in its composition is an intellectual as well as an emotional achievement.

Verse 4 establishes the tree and wood imagery which provides some of the poem's inner coherence. Where other elegies, notably in Old English, find solace in gnomic generalisation — 'swa þes middangeard / ealre dogra gehwam dreoseð ond fealleþ' (thus this earth every single day declines and falls), as *The Wanderer* (62b-63) puts it — *Sonatorrek* achieves a therapeutic distancing of grief through the defamiliarisation inherent in making metaphors. The different components of grief are transmuted in form, yet the patterning of imagery helps to make sense of the bewildering experience of grief and loss.

Þvít ætt mín	For my kin
á enda stendr,	stands at its end,
hræbarnir	beaten into corpses

sem hlynir marka.   like the forest maples. $4^{1\text{-}4}$

Dead or bereaved humans are frequently juxtaposed with
trees in both Old Norse and Old English poetry —
examples include Guðrún's comparison of herself to an
aspen stripped of its branches in *Hamðismál* 5, the
unprotected fir tree in *Hávamál* 50 and tree images in the
Old English *Exeter Maxims* ll. 25b-26, 33 and *Fortunes of Men*
ll.5b-6. In none of these poems is the imagery as highly
developed as in *Sonatorrek*, where this metaphor is
modulated and restated in several stanzas. In v. 5, Egill
returns in memory to his first family loss, the deaths of his
parents, but, with a growing sense that his poetry-making is
not in vain, he succeeds in revivifying the dead wood, his
'kynvið' (kin-wood) 21^{7}, so that it bursts into leaf once more
through the power of his words:

Þat berk út	that I carry out
ór orðhófi	from the temple of words
mærðar timbr	the timber of praise
máli laufgat.	leafy with speech. $5^{5\text{-}8}$

The family is a wooden fence, 'frændgarði', 6^{4}, a
protective enclosure, which the sea has violated by
drowning Bǫðvarr, tearing out a paling, 'hlið' 6^{1}. Egill feels
himself to have been mistreated, 'ryskt' (roughly handled)
by the sea goddess Rán: his indignant sense of violation
becomes apparent in v. 7:

sleitt marr bǫnd	the sea has cut the bonds
minnar ættar,	of my race,
snaran þǫtt	a strong strand
af sjǫlfum mér.	of me myself. $7^{5\text{-}8}$

Egill's sense that an outrageous wrong has been committed
against him personally, emphasised by 'minnar ættar' and
'sjǫlfum mér', brings the desire for a counter-attack: the
same concern with justice and repayment which took such a
positive form in *Arinbjarnarkviða* here demands revenge.
Financial recompense — even if such payment were
possible from the sea goddess — will not do, for a man who

accepts rings for his brother's corpse, 'bróður hrer / við baugum selr' 13^{7-8}, is a betrayer of his kin. No, Egill must have blood-revenge, but then, slowly, as the poem's logical processes grind onwards, he realises that such revenge could only be hypothetical: 'ef vega mættak, / fórk andvígr / ok Ægis mani' (if I could have fought, I would have gone in opposition against the beloved of Ægir [the sea god]) 8^{6-8}. The past subjunctive closes off any prospect of honourable revenge; rather the hopelessness of the endeavour brings another tone to Egill's voice, this time, that of self-pity. With perhaps justifiable hyperbole he dramatises himself as a pathetic, impotent old man — a portrait which emerges more clearly in the later chapters of the saga:

Því alþjóð	for there comes before
fyr augum verðr	the eyes of everyone
gamals þegns	the old man's
gengileysi.	lack of support. 9^{5-8}

It is the public exposure as powerless and vulnerable which hurts Egill here, for something of his old arrogance, his Starkaðr-like misanthropy and disdain for the common folk remains. One of Boðvarr's most praiseworthy characteristics, in Egill's eyes at least, was his loyalty to his father, supporting him, even when the whole people said otherwise: 'þótt oll þjóð / annat segði' 12^{3-4}. This was not the stuff of a bad man, 'vasa ills þegns / efni vaxit' 11^{3-4}. Egill now remembers his brotherlessness; Þórólfr, long dead, is still missed, absent from Egill's side in battle. The phrase 'hverr mér hugaðr / á hlið standi / annarr þegn' (what other man would stand brave by my side) 14^{1-3}, so reminiscent of *Arinbjarnarkviða*, reminds us to how great an extent Arinbjǫrn took over Þórólfr's role for Egill, yet Egill denies him a place in the roll-call of kin. Friends, by the tenets of this poem, cannot replace brothers, but even so 'vinir þverra' (friends are diminishing) 14^8.

    A series of oppositions, of 'them' against 'us', has now been established: those within the 'frændgarði' against the 'alþjóð' outside; Egill and his loyal sons against 'ǫll þjóð'; Egill alive and excluded while all his dead kinsmen, gather in Valhǫll, 'Bileygs í bœ' (in the Weak-sighted One's dwelling) 18[5-6]. In each case, Egill's attempts to differentiate his kin from the common people, to define an exclusive 'in-group' where he belongs, are foredoomed by the death of parents, brother and sons: I think we are not wrong to sense, at this stage in the poem, a growing sense of paranoia on Egill's part as each of these attempts to establish a clan fails.

It is not in Egill's nature to make common cause with the 'alþjóð'; he rejects the popular wisdom of v. 17 which suggests that the best way to assuage sorrow at the loss of a son is to father another. Óðinn acts thus when Baldr is killed, (Baldr's death is an ominous harbinger of *Ragnarǫk*, a theme made prominent in the increasingly eschatological kennings towards the end of *Sonatorrek*), but Egill finds himself more akin to Hreðel, and the Old Man to whom he is compared, in *Beowulf*. He will not, or cannot, produce another son. Nor is other human company pleasing to him (indeed was it ever?):

Erumka þekkt	I am not made happy
þjóða sinni,	by the company of men,
þótt sér hverr	even though each one
sátt of haldi.	may keep the peace. 18[1-4].

The social centre of Egill's life has constituted itself elsewhere; his kin have travelled 'á munvega' (on the paths of delight) 10[6] to Valhǫll and left him alone to grieve. Ægir, lord of ale-brewing, 'fens hrosta hilmir' (prince of the mash of malt) 19[1,3] and 'ǫlsmiðr' (ale-craftsman) 8[3], ironically enough, has brought it about that his son is drinking ale where Egill cannot yet join him.

The fate of Gunnarr, Egill's second son, killed by disease, is alluded to only briefly. Both sons, we learn, were cautious with words, respecting their inherent power which Egill is now unleashing: Bǫðvarr heeded only what his father said, 12[1-2], while Gunnarr was:

at varnaði	on his guard
vamma varr	wary of faults
við vámæli.	against vicious speech. 20^{6-8}

This is Egill's last look back at his lost sons; now his thought turns to the cause of his wrongs. In the past Óðinn has been upholder of the ash-tree of his race, 'ættar ask' 21^4, and his 'kynvið' (kin-wood), but now he replaces Ægir and Rán as the villain: he should have protected Egill's clan, yet he patently failed to do so. Egill had relied on Óðinn: 'gerðumk tryggr / at trúa hánum' (I made sure to trust him) 22^{3-4}. The lines seem to echo *Hávamál* 110^{1-3}, (a poem surely known to Egill, as Klaus von See suggests), although the *Hávamál* verse offers a warning against trusting the god, even when he has sworn a solemn oath:

Baugeið Óðinn	A ring oath
hygg ek at unnit hafi;	I thought Óðinn had sworn;
hvat skal hans	how can his pledge
tryggðom trúa!	be trusted!

Do vv. 21-23 permit us to interpret *Sonatorrek* as a poem about faith and doubt, chronicling a religious crisis, as Nordal and Turville-Petre both suggest? The question is debateable (and indeed much debated), but I feel we should be wary of imputing modern religious sensibilities to a pagan Icelander, given the paucity of our knowledge about pagan cult and belief. The best course here may be to accept Egill's sense of betrayal by Óðinn primarily as a rhetorical device, intensifying the poet's loneliness and alienation from his remaining earthly ties.

Thus, 'því', 23^1, Egill continues to sacrifice to the god, for, he now understands, Óðinn, friend of Mímr, (the severed head which Óðinn consulted to gain wisdom), has given him 'bǫlva bœtr, / ef et betra telk' (recompense for evil, if I reckon up the better aspect) 23^{7-8}. Flawless poetic skill, intelligence, and discernment:

ok þat geð,	and such a spirit
es ek gerða mér,	that I made for myself,

vísa fjándr	certain enemies
af vélǫndum	out of hidden deceivers 24[5-8]

are Egill's gifts from his god, the enemy of the wolf , 'ulfs
bági' 24[2]. With the last three stanzas come an increasingly
eschatological series of kennings for Óðinn. He is no longer
characterised as the thief of the mead of poetry, as in the
early verses of *Sonatorrek*, but rather as the doomed
protagonist of *Ragnarǫk*, desperately consulting Mímr as the
forces of evil advance, and fighting Fenrir, the wolf alluded
to in both 24 and 25. Waiting for death (Hel) on the
headland where his father and brother are buried, Egill
concludes his poem with an extraordinary serenity, in the
face of cosmic and individual destruction:

skalk þó glaðr	yet I shall gladly	
með góðan vilja	with a good will	
ok óhryggr	and unafraid	
heljar bíða.	wait for Hel.	25[5-8].

The power of poetry to bring deeply-felt, private grief
to light, despite the apparent hopelessness of the
endeavour, to bring relief to the anguished mind, to
distance the sorrow by the very act of putting it into words,
and to resolve both emotional and intellectual conflict is
the subject of *Sonatorrek*; a poem which is a process as much
as a completed work of art. At its end, Egill resolves to wait
for death in his own time, for he has found a way of living
with his sorrow. In a clear-sighted calculation of his
advantages, he achieves the balance of loss and gain. The
poetry, in the end, outweighs both the pain and the (self)
pity.

Hǫfuðlausn comes at the mid-point of *Egils saga*,
demonstrating, through its virtuoso use of kenning and
metaphor, the basis for Egill's renown. This essay, I hope,
has shown that it is on the praise-poem *Arinbjarnarkviða*, an
early, and in the warmth of its personal feeling unusual
exemplar of one of the most fertile genres in early Norse
poetry, and on the *Sonatorrek*, a poem of unparalleled
psychological depth, poetic self-awareness and verbal

complexity, that Egill Skalla-Grímsson's reputation as the greatest of all scalds finally deserves to rest.

'Good men' and peace in *Njáls saga*

Judith Jesch
University of Nottingham

Of the many memorable scenes in *Njáls saga*, one of the most striking is in Ch. 116. Its protagonists are a woman called Hildigunnr and her uncle Flosi. Hildigunnr's husband, Hǫskuldr Þráinsson, has been killed by the sons of Njáll, egged on by the evil Mǫrðr Valgarðsson. The killing has universally been condemned and legal proceedings have been instituted. Hildigunnr's uncle Flosi is her nearest male relative. He is disturbed at the news and has been gathering support for the assembly, but has not come out with what he intends to do there.

    When Flosi arrives at the farm, he is greeted enthusiastically by his niece. She offers him the high-seat, which he angrily refuses. When the time comes to wash hands before eating, Hildigunnr gives Flosi a tattered cloth to dry his hands on, which he throws down, using a piece of the tablecloth instead. While Flosi and his men are eating, Hildigunnr comes in, pushing her hair from her face and weeping. Flosi says to her, 'You are heavy-hearted now, kinswoman, since you are weeping, but it is right that you should weep for a good man'. Her reply is to ask whether he will undertake the prosecution or offer her other support. Flosi answers that he will press her claim to the full extent of the law or 'accept such terms of settlement that good men can see that we are fully honoured by it in all respects.' She replies that Hǫskuldr would have taken vengeance for Flosi, had it been his place to do so. After an angry exchange, Hildigunnr takes up from her chest the cloak Hǫskuldr had been wearing when he was killed, flings it over her uncle so that the dried blood rains down on him and makes a formal demand for blood vengeance: 'I call on God and all good men to witness that, by all the powers of

your Christ, and by your manhood and valour, I charge you
to avenge all the wounds he had on his dead body, or else
be called a coward by everyone'.

Flosi responds with one of the best-known mottoes of
saga literature, 'cold are the counsels of women', but he
takes up the challenge. His pursuit of vengeance leads him
down a long path of blood to the burning in their house of
Njáll, his wife, sons and a grandson, and ultimately to the
deaths of those who burned them. Many deaths occur
before the final reconciliation between Flosi, representing
the burners, and Kári, son-in-law of Njáll, who in his turn
took vengeance on them. The saga comes to an exhausted
finish with the marriage of Kári to Hildigunnr.

I chose to begin by looking closely at Ch. 116 for two
reasons. Firstly, because it summarises the three ways
(within the world of the saga) in which it is possible to
achieve redress for a killing: by means of the law, by a
private settlement (both mentioned by Flosi) and by means
of blood vengeance (which is Hildigunnr's preference).
Like most Íslendingasögur, *Njáls saga* rings the changes on
these three methods of resolving a conflict. However, it is
only when vengeance has been stretched to its fullest extent
that the story can end. Secondly, this passage uses the
expression 'good man' or 'good men' three times within a
very short space. It occurred to me to ask what is meant by
this expression and whether it has any connection with the
major theme of resolving conflicts.

To begin with the minor theme. The adjective 'good',
in Old Icelandic as in most languages, has such a wide
range of meanings that it can be difficult to pin down more
precisely than as a general term of approbation, particularly
when applied to people. The interpretation of such words
must rely fairly heavily on the context in which they are
used, both the immediate context and the larger discourse.
The three examples of 'good man/men' in Ch. 116 display
different shades of meaning which are deepened by
resonances elsewhere in the saga or even outside it.

I translated the first example as 'it is right that you
should weep for a good man', yet most translators give 'a
good husband' for this. Both 'man' and 'husband' are of
course perfectly valid translations of *maðr*, but which one we

choose affects the shade of meaning conveyed by the
accompanying adjective. If Hǫskuldr was a 'good husband',
then it is primarily in his relationship to his wife that he is
being seen. If we translate this as a 'good man', then it is a
quality within Hǫskuldr himself that is being emphasised,
independent of his relationships with other people. It
would of course be natural for both Hildigunnr and her
uncle to see the death of Hǫskuldr in the personal terms of
her own loss. The immediate context would thus seem to
require the translation 'a good husband'. Yet if we look at
the larger context of the saga, we find that, while there is
nowhere any indication of what Hildigunnr thought of her
husband, there is plenty of evidence that he was regarded
by the community at large as a 'good man'. The use of this
phrase about Hǫskuldr echoes a previous use of it in Ch. 94,
when we first meet Hǫskuldr (apart from a brief notice of
his birth). In Ch. 94 he is a small boy. His father Þráinn has
just been killed by the sons of Njáll, ostensibly for repeating
some defamatory verses. Njáll has paid compensation for
the death of Þráinn and wishes to foster the fatherless boy,
presumably to cement the reconciliation. The scene in Ch.
94 shows Njáll offering the boy a gold ring and asking if he
knows how his father died. Hǫskuldr answers that he knows
that Njáll's son Skarpheðinn killed him, but adds that 'we
do not need to speak of that which has been settled and for
which full compensation has been paid'. Njáll's reply to this
is 'the answer is better than my question and you will be a
good man'. Coming from Njáll, this has the force of a
prophecy.

    Apart from these two statements, the idea of Hǫskuldr
as a 'good man' is further developed in the manner of his
death. He is, like his father before him, struck down by
Skarpheðinn (Ch. 111). He falls to his knees and cries out
'God help me and forgive you!'. This is a most unusual
manner of death for a saga hero. Hǫskuldr's good qualities
are then posthumously emphasised by the universal
condemnation aroused by his killing. Njáll says that he
would rather have lost two of his own sons than Hǫskuldr.

The district opinion that he was unjustly killed is emphasised in both Ch. 112 and Ch. 115.

Flosi's second use of the phrase 'good men' (in the plural this time) in Ch. 116, however, occurs in a quasi-legal context. He outlines alternative methods of seeking redress for the death of Hǫskuldr, by law or by private settlement. A private settlement must, however, not only do honour to the injured parties, but be seen to do so by 'good men'. These 'good men' confirm the public and quasi-legal nature of the so-called 'private settlement', making it an acceptable alternative to an adjudicated solution. These 'good men' are thus the panels of men which are frequently called upon in the sagas to arbitrate in disputes. This tends to happen when the legal process has for one reason or another come to a halt, but before the antagonists are desperate enough to resort to blood vengeance. Each side in a conflict appoints six men and the panel of twelve arbitrates in balancing the injuries and in deciding the size of compensation to be awarded to the more heavily injured side. This procedure is frequently resorted to in *Njáls saga*, but it must be admitted that settlements reached by these means are not conspicuous for their success in achieving lasting peace. I shall return to these points later.

Finally, Hildigunnr uses the phrase 'good men' in her rhetorical imprecation to Flosi, made before 'God and good men'. Here, the context is explicitly Christian, with the reference to 'your Christ', although Hildigunnr seems to be distancing herself from it. The expression 'God and good men' is alliterative and clearly formulaic. Although not paralleled elsewhere in *Njáls saga*, it is known from other texts. A relevant instance is the *Griðamál*, or Truce Speech, known from the Icelandic laws and also recorded in *Heiðarvíga saga* (Ch. 33) and *Grettis saga* (Ch. 72). This is a formal speech in which the potential truce-breaker is warned that he will be "rækr ok rekinn frá Guði ok góðum mǫnnum ǫllum", 'exiled and outcast from God and all good men'. In this formula, then, 'good men' represent the community as a whole. Hildigunnr of course uses this formula for her own purposes, which are quite different from those of the Truce Speech, but she is essentially appealing to the same idea of the community which will judge one's actions.

Thus we are operating with three distinct concepts of a 'good man' or 'men' in Ch. 116: (1) the morally exemplary individual, as personified by Hǫskuldr, (2) the pool of honourable men who will strive to achieve peaceful resolution of conflicts by arbitration and (3) the righteous and law-abiding members of the community who stand beside God in judgement on an individual who breaks the rules. Similarly, it is made clear that there are three ways of resolving conflicts: (1) by law, (2) by private settlement and (3) by blood vengeance. Together, these two scales form a matrix within which we can discover the moral and intellectual ideals which informed the composition of *Njáls saga*.

The rising scale of conflict resolution, or rather of the attempts to resolve conflicts, forms a discernible pattern in *Njáls saga.* It has been said that the author of the saga knew what its last line would say when he wrote the first. It may initially seem to us that it takes an awfully long time for the story to get going and that there are too many unnecessary preliminaries. But looking back when we have read the whole saga, it becomes clear that the saga shows an escalating series of conflicts. The concern seems to be to explore a variety of ways of resolving these conflicts, as expressed in the tripartite model of Ch. 116.

Although *Njáls saga* is often characterised as the legal saga *par excellence*, it is noticeable that purely judicial ways of settling disputes get fairly short shrift. We are not far into the saga when we find out that the use of only recognised procedures at the assembly will not win a case, however just the cause. The very first person we are introduced to in Ch. 1 is the great lawyer Mǫrðr gígja. His skill in the law is useful in dissolving the marriage of his unfortunate daughter Unnr. But when he brings a case at the General Assembly for the recovery of her dowry, he gets nowhere. The simple fact of the matter is that his former son-in-law, Hrútr, is young and strong, and challenges him to a duel which he dare not accept. The case falls by default and Mǫrðr has no more to offer. The dowry is eventually recovered by the teamwork of the two heroes of the saga, Gunnarr, who has courage and physical strength, and Njáll, who has skill in the law. By a complicated legal trick, Hrútr is summoned. Yet, although the case is just (as Hrútr himself as good as admits), it fails on a procedural technicality. But this time the tables are turned. Gunnarr publicly challenges Hrútr to a contest of strength, forcing him to return the money. The case of Unnr's dowry demonstrates very early on in the saga that legal procedures will only work if they are backed up by force; indeed that force (or the threat of its use) can prevail even when legal procedures have failed. Moreover, it seems that force will prevail whether or not the cause in which it is exercised is just.

The union of physical strength and legal skill represented by the co-operation between Gunnarr and Njáll cannot be used as a means of resolving the next major conflict in the saga, since it involves a dispute between their two households. The feud is conducted between their wives Hallgerðr and Bergþóra, and arises out of personal animosity and a struggle for precedence between the two women. In turn, each woman arranges the killing of a member of the other household, starting with the servants and working their way up until family members fall victim. While the two women do their best to escalate the conflict, it is kept in check by the friendship between their husbands. After each killing, Gunnarr and Njáll get together; the one whose household has been diminished assesses the compensation due to him and the other pays it. In fact, the same bag of money goes back and forth between them a few times. This section of the saga shows us the private settlement of a conflict in its purest form: the representative of the perpetrators immediately offers *sjálfdœmi*, or self-judgement, to the representative of the injured party; he in turn assesses the damage eminently reasonably. The killings always take place while the men are away at the General Assembly in the summer. The news is sent to them and they make their settlement there.

It is made clear that this trouble-free method of resolving a dispute is dependent on the friendship that exists between Gunnarr and Njáll. The gradual escalation of the feud puts their friendly settlements to the test in Ch. 45, when the sons of Njáll kill Gunnarr's cousin, Sigmundr

Lambason. Njáll's reaction when he hears the news is to say 'There will be no self-judgement for this killing as things stand'. It is true that he does not immediately offer self-judgement to Gunnarr, but Gunnarr shows great forbearance in not seeking any redress. Finally, three years later, when discussing another matter with Gunnarr, Njáll slips in an offer of compensation and lets Gunnarr decide its size. Then Gunnarr and Njáll agree that there will never be any matter which they cannot decide by agreement between themselves. 'They held to that and were always friends', the saga tells us.

Using a private settlement to resolve a dispute is, however, not always so easy, especially when the disputants are not such good friends as Njáll and Gunnarr. The next chain of conflict is set off when, after a bad harvest, Gunnarr wishes to buy hay and food from a bad-tempered neighbour. Otkell has plenty of both but refuses either to sell it or give it away. The potential conflict is turned into an actual one by Hallgerðr who sends a man to steal the provisions. Gunnarr is keen to avert further trouble by offering Otkell compensation. Otkell is inclined to accept, but the settlement is sabotaged by his malicious friend Skammkell. Gunnarr then resorts to the threat of force again, but trouble is averted by the intervention of wiser men. Now it is Gunnarr who is the injured party because his earlier offer of self-judgement was rejected and he has to be begged to accept self-judgement himself.

The dispute simmers on until Gunnarr is provoked into his first killing. Just before the case comes up at the General Assembly (Ch. 55), Njáll prophesies a career of killing for Gunnarr, but says he will come out of it all right if he avoids two things: he should never kill twice in the same family and he should never go against a settlement made by 'good men', particularly if he ignores the first warning and does kill twice in the same family. When the case against Gunnarr is brought, his opponents fear that he will use the threat of a duel to force them to back off, but Gunnarr explicitly rejects this course of action, preferring the due process of law. Then Njáll points out that both sides have a good case and they both agree to submit to the arbitration of 'good men'. This episode, then, demonstrates the positive role of 'good men' in a case where both sides have good arguments and are honourable men: where the law cannot resolve a conflict, their active intervention can bring about a private settlement.

A horsefight sets off the next series of conflicts and killings involving Gunnarr, and the same method of arbitration by 'good men' is used to settle each stage of the conflict (Chs. 66, 70, 74) until the final settlement in which Gunnarr is exiled for three years. His refusal to heed this settlement, despite Njáll's warning, leads to his death in an attack on his home. This section of the saga thus demonstrates the inadequacies of such private settlements even when arbitrated by 'good men': because conflicts can flare up again at the instigation of evil or malicious men, and settlements can be disregarded. As each stage of the conflict is temporarily resolved by a private settlement, the lawsuits at the assembly preliminary to the arbitrated settlement get more and more complicated. As Gunnarr gets more and more deeply embroiled in his series of killings, so Njáll has to find more and more devious legal tricks to pressurise his opponents into accepting an arbitrated settlement.

The death of Gunnarr brings a setback to the relatively peaceful settlement of disputes. This is made clear in Ch. 78. First of all, Njáll admits that there can be no lawsuit for the legal killing of Gunnarr and indicates that he would in any case prefer blood vengeance. Then Gunnarr's ghost is overheard in his grave-mound speaking a verse in which he declares that he would rather die in battle than yield. This marks a turning-point in the saga. From here on, an increasing emphasis is placed on blood vengeance. The efficacy of revenge is immediately demonstrated by Njáll's son Skarpheðinn and Gunnarr's son Hǫgni who kill four of Gunnarr's killers and so frighten the others that they pay compensation. This episode is apparently closed when Gunnarr's son and brother are declared 'out of the saga'. But in order to explore fully the ramifications of blood vengeance as a way of settling disputes, a whole new strand of conflict is introduced between the sons of Njáll and Þráinn Sigfússon, son-in-law of Gunnarr's wife, but also his uncle. This conflict is traced by a slender thread back to the long-running dispute between the two households led by Hallgerðr and Bergþóra, but the author is careful to introduce new reasons for it as well.

Njáll no longer acts as a legal adviser; in fact in Ch. 91 he gives his sons tactical advice, since he sees no way out of the conflict except by fighting. However, when his sons do kill Þráinn, Njáll is responsible for arranging a private settlement with compensation for the killing. He also fosters Þráinn's son Hǫskuldr, as we have already seen. From here on, there is an abortive series of vengeance killings, which appear to satisfy those directly involved, interspersed with settlements and truces, which have the same effect. Yet the irrepressible conflict keeps bubbling up as new people discover their grievance. It seems that a settlement only applies to those people who were a party to it. Anyone who was not present and who feels a grievance will then take revenge, causing the dispute to boil over again. This simmering situation leads to the death of Hǫskuldr Þráinsson, and it is at this point that Flosi gets involved in the case and the stage is set for a major lawsuit at the General Assembly.

At first it seems that disaster has been averted when Njáll offers a private settlement and Flosi is persuaded to agree, provided that 'good men' arbitrate. We are told that "allr þingheimr yrði á þessu feginn", 'the whole of the assembly was pleased at this'. The deliberations of the twelve good men are described in detail. They award a greater compensation for the death of Hǫskuldr than had ever been awarded previously. To ensure the settlement is paid in full and promptly, the twelve contribute to it of their own money. Yet, inexplicably, the whole settlement collapses (Ch. 123) when Flosi takes exception to the gift of a silken gown that Njáll had added to the pile of money awarded.

The usual explanation for Flosi's refusal is that the trailing gown is a feminine garment and Flosi takes it as an insult to his masculinity. This interpretation is supported by the fact that Flosi tries to turn the tables by reminding Njáll of his beardlessness, and the scene degenerates into mutual accusations of effeminacy and therefore cowardice. It is also likely that the garment reminds Flosi of the bloody cloak thrust on him by Hildigunnr and hence of her challenge to him to take blood vengeance. He rises to this challenge by attacking and burning to death Njáll and much of his family in their house. The only male member of the family to escape is Njáll's son-in-law Kári. The rest of the saga is then essentially a duel between Flosi, leader of the burners, and Kári, who sets out to hunt them all down and eventually succeeds.

However, this would not be *Njáls saga* if there were not first a long scene in which both sides gear up to fight the case at the General Assembly. Although the prosecution seems to have a watertight case, Flosi engages a clever lawyer to wreck it. We have, in Chs 142-4, a splendidly dramatic description of the legal toing and froing, as the lawyers for both sides do their utmost to gain the procedural upper hand. This is punctuated by comments on the progress of the case from the massed bystanders, like a Greek chorus. The failure of the prosecution case leads to the great battle of the Althing. Finally, however, a settlement is reached by the arbitration of twelve 'good men', both for the killings in the battle and for those who died in the burning. As a result of this settlement, the burners receive stiff punishments: permanent exile for four of them and three years' exile for Flosi. Kári, however, refuses to be a party to the settlement.

The rest of the saga is a somewhat anticlimactic account of how Kári kills some of his adversaries in Iceland and pursues others to Orkney and Wales, where he kills them. Fifteen of the rest die in the battle of Clontarf. Of all the burners, only Flosi is spared. He makes a pilgrimage to Rome where he receives absolution from the Pope. It is stressed that he had thereby fulfilled all the terms of the settlement, both with respect to exile and to compensation. In the final chapter of the saga, Flosi and Kári are reconciled in Iceland and Kári marries Hildigunnr. If the aim is the final resolution of conflicts, then it would appear that Kári's single-handed and single-minded pursuit of vengeance is ultimately the only successful method of ending a dispute. Such a solution appears to vindicate Hildigunnr's argument that legal measures and private settlements are not enough and that vengeance is the only solution. If we take a brutalist point of view, it is true that when all your adversaries have been wiped out, there can be no further killings and retaliations. This is what Kári appears to have achieved. The resolution of disputes would thus simply be a matter of *Realpolitik*: the strongest will prevail, and in order to prevail one must be strong. This was already anticipated in the much more innocuous disputes over Unnr's dowry. However Gunnarr ultimately failed to prevail, despite his strength, but his *alter ego* Kári succeeds.

However I do not believe that the saga reflects this harsh and pessimistic ethos that I have just outlined. The long and interrelated conflicts of the saga are not an essay in how to achieve peace through war. It is true that the saga does offer rather a negative analysis: the emphasis is entirely on how not to arrive at a peaceful solution. But within this negative paradigm a more positive programme can be perceived, a programme for peace.

It has been usual to view the eponymous hero, Njáll, as a representative of the ethos underlying the saga. Njáll is the great lawyer who pronounces (Ch. 70) that 'Our land shall be built with law, but laid waste with lawlessness', often taken to be the motto of the saga. Turville-Petre went so far as to imply that Njáll represents the views of the author of the saga: 'Much that has been said of Njáll could also be said of the saga itself, and it must reflect its author's views on ethics and philosophy'. In this view, then, the saga was written by someone who not only knew the law well, but who had a stake in its success and who must therefore have been greatly depressed at its failure to bring about peace. For there is no doubt that in *Njáls saga* the law is presented as a failure. It cannot even be used to recover a dowry, let alone to control the warring passions of individuals. The final degradation of the law is at the great battle of the Althing. This makes a mockery of the law that the assembly was meant to be free of armed strife.

If the saga is not just a pessimistic analysis of the failure of the law to promote peace, where do we look for a more positive message? I believe the clue lies not with the lawyer Njáll but in the character of Flosi. If we are looking for a character to be the bearer of the message of optimism, it must be one who survives the killings. Having survived,

Flosi is fully reconciled with his enemy, the otherwise remorseless Kári. Both of these points suggest that Flosi is a character to be admired. What there is to be admired in his character is, I think, summed up at the end of Ch. 158, when we are told that he returned to Iceland when 'he had ... fulfilled all the terms of the settlement, both exile and payment of compensation'.

Flosi is the first major character in the saga to hold to the terms of a settlement. There is first of all a contrast with Gunnarr, whose death was the legitimate result of his refusal to go abroad for the three-year exile stipulated by his settlement (Flosi is also outlawed for three years). In addition, there are repeated references to Flosi's determination to keep to the settlement. When (Ch. 147) Njáll's brother Þorgeirr accepts an individual settlement with Flosi and the burners, he stipulates that 'the agreement ... made at the Althing' should 'be kept in every detail' and Flosi readily gives his promise. In Ch. 149, Flosi addresses his fellow burners, saying 'we must be thinking of going abroad and paying our compensation and fulfilling the conditions of the settlements as honourably as possible'. And finally, as already noted, we are explicitly told when Flosi has fulfilled all the terms of the settlement.

The settlement to which Flosi sticks so scrupulously is the one following the great battle of the Althing. This battle is the low point in the maintenance of peace and desperate measures are needed. The tone is set by Hallr of Síða. He lost a son in the battle but generously agrees to forego compensation if only everyone else would agree to arbitration. He asks Snorri goði to arrange this. Snorri, by his eloquence, persuades everyone except Kári and Njáll's brother Þorgeirr. The arbitration is performed by Snorri and 'other good men with him', to a total of twelve.

It seems that a settlement, arranged by 'good men' who ensure that both sides are fairly treated, and kept by the parties who agree to it, is the key to ending and perhaps even preventing serious conflicts. Before Flosi breaks the vicious cycle, all the previous settlements made by good men in the saga were broken and precipitated further conflict. This development is foreseen by Njáll in his warning to Gunnarr (Ch. 55) not to break a settlement arranged by 'good men'. Immediately, in the next chapter, Njáll suggests a settlement arranged by 'good men', which appears to hold. But when Gunnarr's neighbours set about provoking him again in Ch. 58, there is an explicit reference to this settlement: 'Just because Geirr the Priest and Gizurr the White were humiliated by Gunnarr, it doesn't follow that we would be, too'. In other words, the settlement is being explicitly challenged.

In Ch. 66, after Gunnarr had killed a number of men who had ambushed him, the dispute is settled by the arbitration of good men at the instigation of the chieftain Hjalti Skeggjason, apparently on purely disinterested grounds. But immediately in the next chapter, the settlement is repudiated by one of the attackers, who had been wounded but not killed. He immediately recruits Mǫrðr Valgarðsson and they make an unsuccessful attempt to ambush Gunnarr. Accused of conspiracy against Gunnarr, they in turn accuse him of breaking his pledges of peace and therefore the settlement. This dispute is patched up, but a further ambush leads Gunnarr to kill some more men (Ch. 72), going against the warning not to kill twice in the same family. A settlement is reached for this killing by the arbitration of twelve men (Ch. 74). Njáll repeats his warning to Gunnarr, who promises to keep the settlement. But, as we know, he doesn't, and dies for it.

The next reference to breaking a settlement made by 'good men' comes in Ch. 98 when Lýtingr, the brother-in-law of Þráinn Sigfússon, tries to recruit help to avenge his death by killing Njáll's illegitimate son Hǫskuldr. The son of the dead man himself, Hǫskuldr Þráinsson, refuses to participate, and so does Gunnarr's son Grani, saying 'I'm not going to attack the Njálssons and break a settlement made by good men'. Lýtingr's argument is that he was not a party to the settlement. His killing of Hǫskuldr Njálsson, rather than settling an old conflict, sets off a new chain that leads to the death of Hǫskuldr Þráinsson.

Finally, I have already discussed the settlement for the death of Hǫskuldr made in Chs. 122-4. Njáll requests arbitration and Flosi's father-in-law, Hallr of Síða, urges him to let 'good men' arbitrate. Flosi agrees to this, but then refuses to accept the settlement at the last minute. He has clearly not yet learned his lesson and many men must die before he does.

We must next ask what it is about these 'good men' that makes their participation in settlements so important. It is not simply a legal convention, despite the quasi-juridical look of the procedure: the use of twelve men, the references to them as *dómr* and *dómendr*. In spite of this legal terminology, the private settlement is an extra-judicial procedure, even though it often takes place at the assembly, even within the context of a court case. Private settlements are a literary method of 'dispute processing', not a legal one. They are recognised by the Icelandic law codes, but there are few specific provisions for them: the laws are mainly concerned with their possible legal consequences, for instance where outlawry is made a condition. Furthermore, where the laws refer to arbitrators, they are normally called *sáttarmenn*, or something similar. The term *góðir menn* is not used in the context of private settlements in the laws as far as I can discover. Nor is it commonly used in other sagas, although the practice of resorting to such arbitration is common enough. Thus it seems that the emphatic use of the term *góðir menn* is specific to *Njáls saga* and therefore a clue to its interpretation.

In my analysis of Ch. 116, I pointed to three referents of the term 'good men', one of them being the arbitrators in private settlements, while the other two had Christian connotations (the righteous individual and the community of God and good men). It is to these Christian associations that we must now turn.

There is no doubt that alongside the depiction of conflict between men, whether as individuals or in groups, the other major theme of *Njáls saga* is the acceptance of Christianity in Iceland. I have refrained from mentioning this so far, because at first sight there does not seem to be any obvious connection between these two themes. They run side by side, it is true, and occasionally cross, but the points of contact do not seem to come at significant points in the narrative.

Christianity first impinges on the saga in Ch. 81. Gunnarr's brother Kolskeggr, who did keep to the settlement and chose to go abroad while Gunnarr stayed at home, is baptised in Denmark, we are told, but is almost immediately 'out of this saga'. The next we hear of it is the rather abrupt introduction, in Chs. 100-105, of an account of the conversion of Iceland. Two of the first Icelanders to accept the new faith are said to be Njáll and Hallr of Síða. We are also told that Flosi soon accepts preliminary baptism and that Mǫrðr and his father Valgarðr are strongly opposed to the new faith. Finally, Hjalti Skeggjason is outlawed for blaspheming the old gods, and he and Gizurr the White play an important part in persuading all the Icelanders to accept Christianity at the Althing.

With hindsight, we can see that many of the men most eager to accept Christianity (Njáll, Gizurr, Hjalti, Hallr) are precisely those whose names are most frequently mentioned in connection with arbitration by 'good men'. We can also see that the nature of Hǫskuldr's 'goodness' is essentially a Christian one, although we are never explicitly told of his conversion.

After the account of the Conversion, the references to Christianity come thick and fast. The new religion however apparently does nothing to resolve the moral issues of the major conflict, since both sides profess it. Flosi's religious beliefs are stressed at a number of points: we have seen Hildigunnr's contemptuous reference to them, and he has Mass said just before riding off to burn Njáll and his family, acknowledging in Ch. 128 that 'it is a grave responsibility before God, since we are Christian men ourselves'. Njáll's death occurs in a spirit of Christian resignation (he says to his family 'put your faith in the mercy of God, for He will not let us burn both in this world and the next') and is attended by various Christian signs, especially when the bodies of Njáll and Bergþóra are found quite unmarked by the flames. The burners who are killed at Clontarf die on Good Friday. Finally, Flosi achieves his peace by making a pilgrimage to Rome and receiving absolution from the Pope.

The Conversion thus clearly has an important effect on the lives of individuals, but does not seem to impinge on the structure of the saga within which the main conflict is worked out. The Conversion interrupts the sequence of

events in which Hǫskuldr Njálsson is killed in revenge for
the death of Þráinn by Lýtingr, who is in turn attacked, but
not killed, by the sons of Njáll. Immediately after the
Conversion, Hǫskuldr's illegitimate son Ámundi, who is
blind, miraculously gets his sight back to enable him to kill
Lýtingr. As Miller (1983) has convincingly shown, the death
of Hǫskuldr Þráinsson is a continuation of this feud and
occurs when the sons of Njáll are goaded into taking
revenge for the killing of their half-brother Hǫskuldr. It is
hard to see the Conversion as anything more than an
interruption to this story.

    To bring together the concepts of arbitration of
settlements and goodness in a Christian sense, we need to
look outside the saga, to the 12th-century Icelandic Homily
Book. This collection of vernacular sermons naturally
contains a number of references to 'good men', usually in a
purely Christian sense of 'righteous, behaving according to
Christian principles'. However, in one of the homilies, an
explicit parallel is drawn between Christian behaviour and
legal behaviour. The homily on the Annunciation tells of
the mercy and forgiveness shown by the Mother of God to
those who repent of their misdeeds. It is through her
intercession that God is reconciled with the sinner. This is
explained in language that is entirely borrowed from the
vocabulary of the arbitration of disputes. Further, in a gloss
on the Lord's Prayer, the relationship between the sinner
and God is explained in terms of the secular and legal
relationship between a transgressor and the party he has
injured. In both cases, the settlement comes about through
the judgement of others (priests or 'good men') who decide
what atonement is appropriate. God relies on his priests to
make this judgement, just as men in the world must rely on
the judgement of 'good men' to decide secular redress.

    For me, this passage in an Icelandic homily explains
quite neatly the conjunction of ideas in Ch. 116 of *Njáls
saga*, where secular ideas of conflict resolution and religious
ideas of appropriate behaviour come together. This
conjunction is not recognised by Flosi, nor indeed by any of
the other characters in the saga, with the exception of the
'good man' Hǫskuldr Þráinsson who, even as a child, knew

that a settlement should be adhered to. Hǫskuldr's insight is not recognised by the other characters and it dies with him when he is killed. Flosi does learn his lesson by the end of the saga, that he must bow to the judgement of 'good men', of secular arbitrators, in the same way as he bows to the priests of the Christian Church.

There is not much peace in *Njáls saga.* But this is not surprising since all Íslendingasögur are interested in conflict as a literary subject. When an unavoidable period of peace intrudes into the plot, it is usually dismissed with a brief statement, along the lines of 'and then nothing much happened for a year'. Conflicts, on the other hand, are described in loving detail, as we have seen. Yet if we define peace as the absence of conflict, then we can see that this is the aim towards which they are striving. The interest in conflicts is in how to resolve them, not how to multiply them, although clearly it is literarily most interesting to resolve a multiple conflict. This interest in the resolution of conflict is stronger in *Njáls saga* than in many other sagas. That is again not surprising, since *Njáls saga* is the culmination of a highly distinctive literary genre. Many commentators on the saga have emphasised its dependence on sagas that went before. As Turville-Petre put it, 'The influence of a whole library of earlier sagas can be detected in *Njáls saga*'. Such comments refer primarily to the borrowing of plots, characters and motifs and make *Njáls saga* seem very backward-looking. We can turn this idea on its head and instead see the saga as a critical comment on issues raised in its literary predecessors rather than as a kind of reliquary for their bones. This comment is indirect, for realistic narrative such as that of the sagas is an open mode of writing more suited to raising questions than providing answers. Nor does a literature based on stock motifs of conflict allow much scope for getting rid of that conflict except by ending the tale.

I would not, therefore, like to argue that *Njáls saga* has anything as clear as a message, whether it is the solution I have sketched above or any other. But given that it comes at the end of a long period of literary development in the 13th century, and given that its author must have lived through the turbulent events of that century, we cannot fail to see the saga as the product of mature reflection on the nature of conflict and how to achieve its absence. I like to think of it as a kind of novel of ideas, inviting interpretation. Yes, the historical interest is there. Yes, the interest in conflict as merely a vehicle for entertainment is also there. Yet both are lifted onto the next plane, where every assumption is questioned. Why did historical events happen as they did? And why is there always conflict between men?

Texts

Edition: *Brennu-Njáls saga.* Ed. Einar Ól. Sveinsson. Reykjavík, 1954. (= Islenzk fornrit 12) Translation: *Njal's saga.* Trans. Magnus Magnusson and Hermann Pálsson. Harmondsworth, 1960.

> Þá kom Hildigunnr í stofuna ok gekk fyrir Flosa ok greiddi hárit frá augum sér ok grét. Flosi mælti, 'Skapþungt er þér nú, frændkona, er þú grætr, en þó er þat vel, at þú grætr góðan mann.' 'Hvert eptirmæli skal ek nú af þér hafa eða liðveizlu?' segir hon. Flosi mælti, 'Sœkja mun ek mál þitt til fullra laga eða leita til þeira sætta, er góðir menn sjá, at vér sém vel sœmðir af í alla staði.' Hon mælti, 'Hefna mundi Hǫskuldr þín, ef hann ætti eptir þik at mæla.'

> (At that moment Hildigunn came into the room and went up to Flosi, pushed her hair back from her eyes, and wept. Flosi said, 'You are sad now, kinswoman, you are weeping. It is only right that you should weep over a good husband.' 'What redress will you get me?' she asked. 'How much help will you give me?' 'I shall press your claims to the full extent of the law,' said Flosi, 'or else conclude a settlement which in the eyes of all good men will satisfy every demand of honour.' Hildigunn said, 'Hoskuld would have avenged you with blood if he were in your place now.')

> Hildigunnr lagði þá yfir Flosa skikkjuna; dunði þá blóðit um hann allan. Hon mælti þá, 'þessa skikkju gaft þú, Flosi, Hǫskuldi, ok gef ek þér nú aptr. Var hann ok í þessi veginn. Skýt ek því til guðs ok góðra manna, at ek sœri þik fyrir alla krafta Krists þíns ok

fyrir manndóm ok karlmennsku þína, at þú hefnir sára
þeira, er hann hafði á sér dauðum, eða heitir hvers
manns níðingr ella.'

(She threw the cloak around his shoulders, and the
clotted blood rained down all over him. 'This is the
cloak you gave to Hoskuld, Flosi,' she said, 'and now I
give it back to you. He was wearing it when he was
killed. I call upon God and all good men to witness
that I charge you in the name of all the powers of your
Christ and in the name of your courage and your
manhood, to avenge every one of the wounds that
marked his body – or be an object of contempt to all
men.')

Homíliu-bók. Ed. Theodor Wisén. Lund, 1872.
Die annunciationis beate Marie virginis ac Dei genitricis

Við þann mann hvern vill guð dróttinn sættask, at
kennimanna sinna dómi, es góðra manna dóm vill
þiggja, fyrir allar sakar þær, es menn gera við hann. Vill
guð dróttinn ok eigi sjálfr hefna, heldr vill hann hlíta
þeira manna forráði... Fyrirgef svá þú oss várar syndir,
nú es vér biðjum þik guð dróttinn af ǫllum hug, ok
endum yfirbœtr slíkar es kennimenn þínir bjóða oss,
sem vér fyrirgefum þeim mǫnnum, er afgøra við oss í
þessi verǫldu, ok bjóða oss yfirbœtr slíkar er þeir hafa
til at góðra manna dómi, þá es þeir biðja oss af ǫllum
hug sínum...

(The Lord God wishes to arrive at a settlement,
according to the judgement of his priests, with each
man who wishes to accept the judgement of good men,
for all those wrongs which men do to him. The Lord
God does not wish to take vengeance himself, rather
he wishes to rely on the management of these men...
Forgive us our sins, now that we pray to you Lord God
with all our hearts and perform such penances as your
priests command us, just as we forgive those men who
transgress against us in this world and offer us such
compensation as they have according to the judgement
of good men, when they beg us with all their hearts...)

Women in *Njáls saga*

Heather O'Donoghue
University of Oxford

The women in *Njáls saga* are commanding and compelling
figures, and many scholars have singled them out for critical
attention without any feminist analysis of the saga in mind.
In fact, what fascinates readers and critics about them is just
what seems to halt a feminist analysis in its tracks, for
feminist literary criticism takes as its starting point the way
female characters are marginalized in both literature and
criticism, and the female characters seem far from
marginalized in *Njáls saga*. They are on the contrary very
prominent, and have been well represented in saga
criticism; they include some of the most powerful moving
forces in the saga narrative. In this, and in other ways I shall
discuss, the depiction of the women in *Njáls saga* challenges
our preconceived notions of gender distinction.

Gender distinctions rest on social and cultural
differences between men and women rather than biological
ones — that is, on socially conditioned ideas of what is
"natural" behaviour in men and women. Sociologists claim
that society tends to construct the two genders, masculine
and feminine, as mutually exclusive and opposing
categories. I shall argue that it becomes apparent in *Njáls
saga* that the author does associate the female characters
with a distinctive social role in his narrative, although it may
not be a role we would call a feminine one, and that this is
often in direct opposition to the role the saga author assigns
to his male characters, whose masculinity is in turn re-
defined

The saga does not simply present us with women who
behave like men and vice versa; to claim that its author
depicts as his norm women more "masculine" and men
more "feminine" than a twentieth-century reader of
medieval literature may have come to expect would
highlight cultural differences between readers and text but
would not necessarily indicate that the author was especially

interested in the question of gender. But I hope to show that the saga author insistently explores the theme of gender distinction, both in terms of what characterises the behaviour of each gender, and of how the two are in perpetual conflict.

In her 1980 Dorothea Coke Memorial lecture, "The Role of Sexual Themes in *Njáls saga*", Ursula Dronke offers a masterly analysis of how the saga author, with his extraordinary ability to depict private feelings, could transcend the stereotypical in his account of sexual relationships in the saga. I am greatly indebted to Mrs. Dronke's lecture. Sexual relations between men and women are of course central to masculine and feminine ways of behaving, and much of what I have to say here has its roots in "The Role of Sexual Themes". But I would like to go on to consider social as well as sexual relationships, looking particularly at the exercise of power in society.

The relationship between Unnr, the daughter of Mǫrðr gígja, and Hrútr Herjólfsson seems at first to provide a good example of a woman's lack of independence. Unnr is presented in the saga solely in terms of her marital eligibility. She is conventionally acceptable, good-looking, well brought up: in short, a good match. The men around her — her father, the bridegroom-to-be, Hrútr, and his half-brother Hǫskuldr — organise the betrothal, and we are not told that Unnr herself was consulted in any way. Although Hrútr is given the opportunity to look over Unnr, we are not told when Unnr first sees him. Unnr is presented as being quite powerless in the whole transaction.

When Hrútr goes abroad he meets Queen Gunnhildr, who, in marked contrast to Unnr, is extremely powerful. Gunnhildr is powerful not only by virtue of her social rank as Queen Mother of Norway, but also because of her sexual and domestic independence. The French historian, Georges Duby, has shown how in Western Europe in the Middle Ages, while daughters could be regarded as the property of their fathers, and wives of their husbands, widows achieved a measure of financial and sexual independence which, it seems, male authors may represent as threatening. As a result, such women may be portrayed either as comic figures, such as Chaucer's Wife of Bath, in order to defuse the threat, or as sinister and sexually rapacious power wielders.

Gunnhildr's charged sexual relationship with Hrútr in Norway has been perceptively interpreted in Ursula Dronke's "The Role of Sexual Themes". Here I want to point out that although Hrútr now becomes the object of an imperious and overbearing sexuality, we cannot say that the tables have been turned, and that he is now as powerless as Unnr was. It is more complicated than that, and one important difference is that Unnr's lack of power is unremarkable, given the prevailing social mores, while Gunnhildr's power over Hrútr is seen as sinister and magical, and is ultimately malevolent.

But the saga author does not simply leave us with this rich contrast in social acceptability between male and female sexual power. Unnr was powerless at her betrothal, and is already deceived when she is married. But she has an inner life which the saga author allows her to withhold from us, and from the other characters in the saga. This is hinted at when she is described, without explanation or comment, as low-spirited, "dǫpr", at the wedding feast. We are perhaps reminded of another literary exploration of unexpected shifts in the balance of power in a marriage, as Chaucer's May, apparently the victim of an oppressive marriage to old Januarie in the Merchant's Tale, presents an unreadable countenance on her wedding night: "But God woot what that May thoughte in hir herte / When she hym saugh..."

The public face of Unnr's marriage is in fact very promising, for Hrútr gives her total control over domestic matters, and this is seen as a generous act (Hallgerðr does not presume to take over the running of the joint household of her new husband Glúmr and his brother Þórarinn, for example). However, the marriage is an unhappy one, and in a remarkably perceptive and sympathetic scene, Unnr tries to explain to her father what is wrong, but is intimidated by the men who have arranged the marriage, and finds herself unable to reply when she is directly challenged by Hrútr to cite a complaint.

At the next Alþing, Unnr describes her sexual problem with Hrútr to her father in fully explicit terms: Hrútr's penis becomes, during love-making, too large for

them to consummate their marriage. One assumes that this
is the result of a curse laid on Hrútr by Queen Gunnhildr.

It is striking that while Unnr is not shown to expect
the right to be consulted about her marriage, she
apparently claims the right to sexual satisfaction from her
husband. And Unnr's father Mǫrðr does not hesitate for
one moment about the significance of her complaint — he
doesn't for example try to persuade her that the marriage is
worth saving because of its social and material advantages.
At once, he plans her divorce. Perhaps Unnr never did want
Hrútr for her husband; her silence has put her feelings out
of our reach, as well reflecting her lack of choice and
power.

Hrútr, by a grotesque contrast, has in a sense been
over-endowed with sexual power. One might have expected
a jealous lover's curse to make a man impotent; Gunnhildr's
punishment is almost ironic, an oddly appropriate
reflection of her own strong and open sensuality.

Unnr's inscrutability is now used to shift dramatically
the balance in power in her relationship with Hrútr. She
pretends affection for him, and feigns illness; Hrútr is
defenceless, and shows touching solicitude. When she
divorces herself from him, it is his turn to take refuge in
silence.

Hrútr's magnanimity when children are caught
laughing at his humiliating inability to consummate the
marriage (and it's not clear from the wording in the saga
that they are not just sniggering at what they suppose to be
impotence — a simple lack of virility rather than Hrútr's
bizarre excess of it) shows Hrútr's moral and social self
triumphing in the face of mockery about his sexuality. The
social aspect of his masculinity — he is praised for his
"drengskapr" (manliness) — is asserted just as the sexual
one is disparaged.

Like Unnr, Hallgerðr is betrothed without being
consulted about the match. Þorvaldr and his father Ósvífr
approach Hallgerðr's father Hǫskuldr, and the men make a
betrothal agreement. Hallgerðr is told of the betrothal, and
protests both about not being consulted, and about the
quality of the match. She is articulate and sarcastic, but is

not able to refuse. Although she is far from silent at this point, she too, like Unnr, can be inscrutable: Þorvaldr boasts after the wedding that she laughs at his jokes and is affectionate towards him, but he is deceived. Hallgerðr encourages her foster-father to kill Þorvaldr, and her new independence as a widow is perhaps reflected in the rather different betrothal arrangements with her second husband Glúmr: although the men meet initially to discuss the match, Hrútr warns that Hallgerðr must be consulted in due course, and he and his half-brother Hǫskuldr are plainly nervous about the affair. Hallgerðr, on the other hand, is confident and self-possessed, and insists on an exact account of what the men have said so far. Her marriage to Glúmr is successful, if short, and they have a child, whom Hallgerðr names Þorgerðr, after her grandmother.

Hallgerðr behaves impressively in all respects while she is married to Glúmr, and the saga author relates how she loved Glúmr so much that she cannot help crying when they quarrel and he hits her. She seems soft- rather than hard-hearted here. But when her foster-father kills Glúmr, her self-possession is extraordinary and terrifying. She laughs when Þjóstólfr admits to the crime, and sends him off to Hrútr, to his death; and she does it so calmly that his suspicions are barely aroused. Her inscrutability and her temperament give her power over the lives of the men around her.

Hallgerðr's most celebrated relationship is with Gunnarr. The saga author's description of their meeting at the Alþing, with Hallgerðr confident and alluring, no longer hedged about by father and uncle, presents her in the role of the independent widow. She is not sinister or witch-like, but she is a formidable figure all the same, and her male relatives are horrified by Gunnarr's plan to marry her. Hrútr is determined to behave honourably (even if Hǫskuldr seems prepared to take the opportunity offered to get rid of Hallgerðr), and his account of Hallgerðr's flaws of character very nearly has the desired effect of putting Gunnarr off the marriage.

The men are concerned not only on Gunnarr's account, that he is making a marriage which may prove unhappy, but also because of the disruptive effect such a marriage may have on social relations. Njáll responds in a similar way: "Af henni mun standa allt it illa, er hon kemr austr hingat" ('She will be the cause of nothing but trouble if she comes here to the east'). Hallgerðr is regarded as a potential source of unspecified disturbance, a socially disruptive power against which the men must unite and struggle to preserve some stability in their society.

When Bergþóra, Njáll's wife, is introduced in the narrative, she is described, like Hallgerðr, as "skaphǫrð" (hard-hearted). But unlike Hallgerðr, she is not seen to be sexually attractive, and the saga author calls her "drengr góðr", a term normally used of men, and rather rarely of women (though it is also used of Hildigunnr in this saga), which might be translated as "a fine person" or even "a manly person"; plainly she is not conventionally feminine. Although she and Njáll have three sons, Njáll has another son by Hróðný, and the saga author tells us little about Njáll's relationship with her (what evidence there is in the saga is illuminatingly interpreted in "The Role of Sexual Themes"). But we cannot help seeing Bergþóra slightly differently in the light of it.

When Bergþóra and Hallgerðr quarrel, setting in train the dreadful series of revenge murders, there is no clear moral distinction drawn between the two of them; they engage in the feud with equal determination and cold-bloodedness. Bergþóra herself initiates the ill-feeling with her curt demand that Hallgerðr give precedence to Þórhalla, the wife of their youngest son: "Þú skalt þoka fyrir konu þessi" ('Move down to make room for this woman'). But just as we remember Hallgerðr above all for her fierce denial of help to Gunnarr when he is attacked by his enemies, and are inclined to overlook her happy marriage to Glúmr, so Bergþóra's unswerving loyalty to Njáll at the burning dominates our impression of her, and we are inclined to see her as an exemplary wife in direct contrast to Hallgerðr .

Hildigunnr is the third of these fierce, powerful and vengeful women in *Njáls saga*, and the saga author uncompromisingly describes her as "allra kvenna grimmust ok skaphǫrðust ok drengr mikill" (the fiercest and most hard-hearted of all women, and a fine [*or even* manly] person). She refuses to marry Njáll's illegitimate son, Hǫskuldr, until Njáll manages to provide him with the status of a chieftain, and the saga author makes no comment at all on the personal aspects of their marriage. Hildigunnr takes the centre stage — with magnificent theatricality, as Ursula Dronke points out — when she successfully persuades her uncle Flosi to avenge the death of Hǫskuldr. But even here, she does not claim to be moved by grief and affection for her dead husband, but rather by a single-minded desire for revenge.

Savage determination that wrongs must be avenged, that insults should never be forgotten and that lethal violence is the only proper response to threats to one's pride and honour are shown in *Njáls saga* to be women's work. The men are unwilling to be drawn in; Flosi berates Hildigunnr's demand for revenge, calling her a monster and adding "eru kǫld kvenna ráð" (female advice is devoid of feeling, *and/or*, lethal). Skarpheðinn Njálsson, himself a fighting man, is infuriated by Hallgerðr's joke about his own father's effeminacy, but implies that stoicism is more manly than anger: "Ekki hǫfu vér kvenna skap...at vér reiðimsk við ǫllu" ('We are not women to fly into a rage about everything'). Njáll himself responds to Bergþóra's goading with remarkable restraint; although he does not rule out vengeance, he asserts that "jafnan orkar tvímælis" (there are always two sides to a case). The women in the saga are far from being the peace weavers feminist critics claim to identify in the Old English heroic tradition; it is the men who negotiate arbitration and settlement, who try to do things properly in a civilized way according to the new due processes of the law. Nowhere is this made clearer than in the account of Hallgerðr and Bergþóra's lethal feuding; the men are all away at the Alþing in civilized assembly each time the tit-for-tat killings take place.

Throughout the saga, women goad men to violence, from the powerful influence of Bergþóra or Hildigunnr to the determination of a female character who is not even given a name urging Þráinn Sigfússon's brother-in-law to take vengeance for his kinsman. The men try to resist this provocation, as does Grani Gunnarsson on this occasion: "Nei..ekki mun ek fara at Njálssonum ok rjúfa sætt þá, er góðir menn gerðu" ('No...I'm not going to attack the sons of Njáll and break the settlement which good men have made'). Especially striking is a series of provocative remarks by Hildigunnr, the daughter of Starkaðr, who insistently inflames her father and brothers by comparing them unfavourably with Gunnarr of Hlíðarendi; the men are reluctant to engage in either the proposed horse-fighting or the ensuing battle, and they are in the end defeated (though the episode is one of the factors leading to Gunnarr's death). Hildigunnr is not driven by the desire for revenge here; she seems to represent an almost motiveless spirit of disruption and anarchy. Finally, we should not overlook Kormlǫð, the Irish queen regarded by both the Irish and the Viking chieftains as the vengeful instigator of the Battle of Clontarf, at which so many impressive men on both sides were killed.

We can now see the gender division drawn up by the author of *Njáls saga* in a clearer light. Women insist on the old violent, heroic ways of regulating society, ways which tend to run out of control, and which the men are shown to be struggling to replace with settlements and agreements. The saga shows us the tension between women and men as a struggle between the old and the new. When Þangbrandr, the Christian missionary, comes into the saga, his new faith is dramatically opposed by a woman, Steinunn, who in two skaldic verses asserts the power of Þórr against that of Christ, and articulates in the old pagan medium a fierce challenge to social change. Þangbrandr is silenced by the outburst.

So what of the men most closely involved with the powerful women in *Njáls saga*? Gunnarr and Njáll are the twin protagonists in the narrative, and both show distaste for the old violent ways, and question how a man should behave. Gunnarr has none of the cold single-mindedness of the saga's female characters. He falls in love with Hallgerðr at first sight, making a disastrous marriage; he again allows his emotions to override his judgement in the celebrated scene in which he refuses to take the prudent course of exile from Iceland because he is suddenly overcome by how beautiful his home, Hlíðarendi, looks. Most significantly, he ponders his masculinity, because he doesn't like killing: "Hvat ek veit," segir Gunnarr, "hvárt ek mun því óvaskari maðr en aðrir menn sem mér þykkir meira fyrir en ǫðrum mǫnnum at vega menn" ('I'd like to know' says Gunnarr, 'whether I must be less manly than other men, because for me, killing is a bigger thing than for other men').

For a time, Njáll is a more successful example of what we might call "the new man". Like Gunnarr, he too dislikes violence and the old heroic imperatives, but finds power in the structures of civilization, primarily, of course, in the law. But although the saga narrative for a while holds in equilibrium the opposing forces of vengeance and reconciliation, violence and arbitration, women and men, what at last tips the balance is the insult of effeminacy.

The women lace their goading throughout the saga with accusations of effeminacy against the men. Hildigunnr threatens that Flosi's manhood will be a matter for public doubt if he won't avenge the death of Hǫskuldr. Hallgerðr derides Njáll and his sons as "karl inn skegglausa ... ok taðskegglinga" (Old Beardless and the Little Dungbeards), and this insult is repeated by Bergþóra, although it fails to rouse Skarpheðinn to immediate action (as discussed above, Skarpheðinn dismisses sudden anger as "kvenna skap"). It recurs ominously in the narrative until Flosi, himself goaded by the settlement gift of a garment which could be worn by either a man or a woman, throws it back at Skarpheðinn and the hard-won settlement for the murder of Hǫskuldr is destroyed.

The effeminacy insult in *Njáls saga* has of course lost logical force given the saga author's re-drawing of gender distinctions — if the men did behave like women there would be swifter vengeance and more corpses. But it seems that the accusation of what is seen as sexual "perversion", men behaving like women in sexual, rather than social, terms, retains its deadly power. Both within the world of the saga, and as a narrative climax in the text, it is entirely fitting that the wrecking of a legal settlement should be achieved with sexual insults.

Saga authors famously purport to tell "what happened", to relate in a naturalistic mode a plausible reconstruction of an actual world. But the author of *Njáls saga*, as well as producing this naturalistic illusion with extraordinary skill, goes one step further in using his narrative to explore and exemplify certain themes; among them, the power struggle between the two genders. We can be confident that this is part of the saga author's creative purpose, because of the way the whole narrative is imbued with variations on the theme, is even, one might claim, constructed around it. The saga opens with a profound and subtle exploration of power shifting between a man and a woman in a sexual and social relationship. And just as the primary narrative climax, the burning of Njáll and his family, is precipitated by gibes about effeminacy, so at the burning itself, the saga author concerns himself with the play of gender.

Bergþóra, a wife who is courageously and steadfastly loyal to her marriage bond, refuses to leave Njáll and is burnt alongside him in the house. In this, she shares the fate not only of her husband, but also of the men in general, for the women, whom she declines to join, are allowed out. We may feel here an echo of the old heroic loyalty along with the more obvious marital one. But at the same time, one of Njáll's sons performs exactly the opposite manoeuvre. Helgi (significantly recalling his namesake in the *Edda*, Helgi Hundingsbani) dresses in his sister-in-law's clothes, and makes his exit with the women.

"It seemed to me that the sweetest light of my eyes had been extinguished"

Andrew Hamer
University of Liverpool

Imagery and *metaphor* are terms already familiar to students when they begin the study of the sagas. And yet discussion in British university classes of the literary qualities of the sagas seldom focuses upon the function of metaphor, a fact which may well be surprising to those students who are aware that the sagas were produced by the same culture that also maintained and preserved scaldic poetry.

The reason for the exclusion of metaphor from the literary study of the sagas is quite simply the belief among scholars that 'saga style' is alien to the employment of this and other related rhetorical devices. Richard F. Allen's influential book *Fire and Iron: Critical Approaches to Njáls saga* (1971) states the standard critical position confidently and succinctly (p.12): "The epithets, similes, and metaphors which provide for so many critics useful entries into a work and which again mark much oral narrative are not found in the sagas. Figurative language is rare in saga prose, although all the more telling when it occurs."

Njáls saga would appear to offer the reader a good opportunity to test whether saga style is in fact inimical to different sorts of figurative language. A large body of critical writing on the saga has established that the anonymous author was widely read in vernacular Icelandic literature, including, for example, other sagas of Icelanders and an account (or accounts) of the coming of Christianity to Iceland; he seems also to have known some works of foreign origin which were available in Icelandic translations, including some saints' lives and the popular *Dialogues* of Gregory the Great. Since the use of metaphor is a common feature in these texts, the author of *Njála* may well have been familiar with its nature and purpose.

Two questions therefore provide the starting point for the present essay. Firstly, would an Icelander, quite possibly without any formal training in rhetoric, have identified the function of such elements of figurative writing as "epithets, similes and metaphors"? Secondly, does he use any of the same elements in his own work? A positive answer to the second question, while not actually presupposing a positive answer to the first — it cannot be proved that the author of *Njála* had read these translations of Latin texts — does nevertheless strongly suggest that he had recognised in his reading the narrative role played by these figurative elements. This paper will concentrate on one of these elements, metaphor, treating it as a test-case for the use in the sagas of figurative language.

The words of Njáll which form the title of this paper are uttered at the Althing that follows the killing of Hǫskuldr Hvítanessgoði (Ch. 122): 'þótti mér slǿkkt it sǿtasta ljós augna minna". These words mark one of the most tense moments in the saga: the law-suit following Hǫskuldr's death has reached deadlock; the attempts of Njáll and his sons to gain support from powerful chieftains have been to a large extent frustrated by Skarpheðinn's "over-ready tongue"; and a peaceful outcome, though widely longed-for at the Althing, would appear to be almost impossible to effect. At this moment, the saga author puts a metaphor into the mouth of Njáll.

Lars Lönnroth (*Njáls Saga: A Critical Introduction*, pp.113-4) is quite clear in his own mind about the status of these words: "This is not saga language. As Sveinsson has shown, the expression emanates from the Vulgate. David uses the same metaphor when he feels estranged from God: 'even the light of my eyes has left me'". Lönnroth goes on to suggest that the phrase "light of my/our eyes" is used in medieval hagiography by bereaved parents, mourning "the loss of a beloved and saintly child". That the saga author has Njáll use this metaphor to describe his feelings over the loss of his foster son suggests that he was entirely familiar with this hagiographic formula of the bereaved parent. But he departs from the tradition in placing the formula not as part of an immediate response to the news of the saintly child's death, but within the context of his comment on the inability of law to act (Ch. 122): "Svá sýnisk mér sem þetta mál sé komit í ónýtt efni, ok er þat at líkendum, því at af illum rótum hefir upp runnit". ('It seems to me that this case has reached deadlock; and that is scarcely surprising, for it has grown from an evil deed'.)

Njáll's words here continue a theme which had been stated in chapter 97, where, as a result of Njáll's manipulation of the law, a whole series of law-suits becomes deadlocked:

> Þetta sumar váru þingdeildir miklar; gerði þá margr sem vant var at fara til fundar við Njál, en hann lagði þat til mála manna, sem ekki þótti líkligt, at eyddusk sóknir ok svá varnir, ok varð af því þræta mikil, er málin máttu eigi lúkask, ok riðu menn heim af þingi ósáttir.

> (There was heavy litigation that year, and as usual many people came to consult Njal; but Njal, against all likelihood, gave them advice which each time led to deadlock between plaintiff and defendant. Bitter quarrels arose when legal agreement could not be reached, and people rode home from the Althing with their differences unsettled.)

Njáll engineers the paralysis of these law-cases in order to point out the necessity for a Fifth court, a court of appeal, the establishment of which by the Court of Legislature leads directly to Njáll's desired goal of creating a chieftainship for Hǫskuldr. It is the securing of this chieftainship which in turn enables Hǫskuldr to marry Hildigunnr and, since she is the niece of Flosi, will later place Flosi under obligation to prosecute Hǫskuldr's killers.

Following Hǫskuldr's death, metaphorically the extinguishing of the light of Njáll's eyes, the process of law is once again incapacitated, and the resulting court-hearing reaches deadlock. This paper differs from the views of Einar Ólafur Sveinsson and Lars Lönnroth in claiming that the words spoken by Njáll form merely one example, albeit a powerful one, of what is a recurrent metaphor in *Njáls saga*, a metaphor of vision which defines the success or otherwise of the process of law according to how clearly those characters who seek justice are able to see. A brief episode early in the saga sets up the paradigm for the operation of the metaphor: in chapter 12, Hallgerðr's foster father Þjóstólfr murders her first husband, Þorvaldr, and is sent by her for refuge to her uncle Svanr, a man "extremely skilled in witchcraft". A *posse comitatus*, led by Þorvaldr's father Ósvífr, pursues Þjóstólfr, but the hunters are baffled by Svanr's magic:

> Nú er frá því at segja, at þeir Ósvífr riðu á hálsinn ok menn hans; þá kom þoka mikil í móti þeim ... Litlu síðar sé sorti mikill fyrir augu þeim, svá at þeir sá ekki.

> (Meanwhile, Osvif and his men were riding over the hill when a thick bank of fog advanced to meet them ... A little later a great darkness descended on them, blinding their eyes.)

The pursuit is aborted, and Þjóstólfr escapes justice, a particularly ironic conclusion since the pursuit had started confidently in the right direction, guided by Ósvífr's clarity of insight:

> "sé ek nú allt eptir, hversu farit hefir. Hallgerðr mun sent hafa Þjóstólf til Bjarnarfjarðar ... Skulum vér nú safna liði ok sœkja hann norðr þangat."

> ('I can see what must have happened after the killing. Hallgerd will have sent Thjostolf to Bjarnarfjord ... We shall now gather a force and go north after Thjostolf.')

This episode may be compared with the events narrated in chapter 88, which details the escape from Norway of Víga-Hrappr. Lönnroth, *op. cit.* pp.134-6, treats these two parallel episodes thematically as examples of a 'folk motif: a person's miraculous escape'; once again, however, as with the motif of the loss of a saintly child discussed earlier, we see the saga author working with traditional materials to further the development of his metaphor. Hrappr, guilty of seduction, manslaughter, and the looting of a pagan temple half-owned by the pious Earl Hákon, is an outlaw with a price on his head. He flees, and is concealed in a succession of different hiding-places on board the boat of Þráinn Sigfússon. Three times, the earl very nearly discovers Hrappr, but on each occasion is only able to 'see' his hiding-place too late, by which time Hrappr is already concealed elsewhere; the earl's pagan piety gives him a degree of supernatural insight which is just too little to allow him to defeat the alliance of Hrappr and Þráinn Sigfússon, an alliance which will later, in Iceland, prove socially disruptive and ultimately self-destructive.

Þjóstólfr's destruction comes as a result of his murder of Hallgerðr's second husband, Glúmr (chapter 17). Hallgerðr is in love with this man, however, and sends Þjóstólfr to the home of her uncle Hrútr Herjólfsson, the saga implying that by so doing she is sending him to execution. This time, despite the fact that once again Þjóstólfr is protected by darkness — he arrives at Hrutstead during the night — Hrútr, as Hallgerðr's intended executor of justice, is for some reason already vigilant, and is able to make his way unerringly towards Þjóstólfr: "Hann gekk norðr um vegginn ok sá þar mann mikinn ok kenndi, at þar var Þjóstólfr"(He walked north round the house and caught sight of a tall figure. He realized that it was Thjostolf.)

Þjóstólfr's earlier escape from Ósvífr's pursuit had been a simple matter to arrange: "Svanr mælti: 'Gakk þú út með mér; lítils mun við þurfa.'" ('Come outside with me,' said Svan. 'We won't need much for this.') On this first occasion, Þjóstólfr had been pursued by the forces of justice alone, justice unsupported by any other power; Víga-Hrappr, on the other hand, had very nearly been detected by forces of justice powered by the supernatural insight of Earl Hákon. And now, in the third episode discussed, justice does finally catch up with Þjóstólfr. And since Hallgerðr and Hrútr are jointly responsible for Þjóstólfr's death, it is reasonable to conclude that, in this instance, the representative of violence and darkness is destroyed by the clear-sighted combination of justice and marital love.

The figure whose power works most obviously against the operation of marital love is Gunnhildr (chapters 3-6),

whose curse on Hrútr begins the saga's movement into
tragedy. Gunnhildr energises a world of intrigue where
others feel forced to collude with her in secrecy.
Gunnhildr's servant, Ǫgmundr, visits Ǫzurr and Hrútr,
newly arrived in Norway:

> Hann sagði þeim ørendi sín af hljóði. Síðan tǫluðu
> þeir leyniliga ráðagerð sína, ok rœddi Ǫzurr við Hrút:
> "Svá lízk mér, frændi, sem nú muni vit hafa gǫrt ráð
> okkat, því at ek kann skapi Gunnhildar."

> (He gave them the queen's message secretly, and then
> Ozur and Hrut considered it in private. 'It seems to
> me,' said Ozur, 'that our decision is already
> made, kinsman. I know Gunnhild's nature.')

A society like that of Gunnhildr's Norway, based on
secrecy, allows those in power to monopolise and control
the flow of information, and indeed Gunnhildr does appear
to be all-seeing and all-knowing:

> Nú spurðisk skipkváman austr þangat til Víkrinnar. Ok
> þegar er þetta spyrr Gunnhildr, frétti hon eptir, hvat
> íslenzkra manna væri á skipi; henni var sagt, at Hrútr
> hét maðr ok var bróðurson Ǫzurar. Gunnhildr mælti:
> "Ek veit gǫrla: hann mun heimta erfð sína, en sá maðr
> hefir at varðveita, er Sóti heitir."

> (News spread of the arrival in Oslofjord of a ship from
> the west, and as soon as Gunnhild heard of it she
> wanted to know what Icelanders were on board. She
> was told that one of them was Hrut, Ozur's nephew. 'I
> have no doubt at all that he is here to claim his
> inheritance,' said Gunnhild. 'A man called Soti has
> taken charge of it.')

Since information is power, the flow of information
must always work to Gunnhildr's advantage, of course, and
can therefore only be one-way. While she ensures that
information about others reaches her ("En nú haf þú njósn
af ... ok seg mér" — 'And now keep watch ... and let me
know'), she is determined that no information about her
own secrets shall leak out: "þá mælti Gunnhildr við þá

menn, er þar váru: 'þér skuluð engu fyrir týna nema lífinu, ef þér segið nokkurum frá um hagi vára Hrúts." (Gunnhild warned her attendants: 'If you breathe a word about myself and Hrut, it will be your last.')

The secrecy surrounding Hrútr's sexual liaison with Gunnhildr is ironically contrasted with the cruelly open mockery of his unconsummated marriage (chapter 8). Yet it is precisely at this moment of public ridicule, when darkness and secrecy, degradation and self-destruction seem to dominate the saga, that positive, socially integrative forces begin to act, and Hrútr's moral rehabilitation occurs under the test of public scrutiny. He addresses the boy who has been mocking him:

> "Gakk hingat til mín." Sveinninn gerði svá. Hrútr dró fingrgull af hendi sér ok gaf honum ok mælti: "Far braut ok leita á engan mann síðan." Sveinninn fór í braut ok mælti: "Þínum drengskap skal ek við bregða æ síðan." Af þessu fekk Hrútr gott orð.

> ('Come over here to me,' said Hrut. The boy did so. Hrut drew a gold ring from his finger and gave it to him. 'Go away now,' he said, 'and never provoke anyone again.' The boy went away saying, 'I shall always remember your noble-mindedness.' Hrut was highly praised for this).

At the same time as it signals Hrútr's own moral re-awakening, the forgiveness which he shows the boy allows the latter an opportunity to amend his treatment of others: "leita á engan mann síðan". Hrútr's words are not weakly sentimental: the forgiveness is stern and demanding, and the boy's reply shows he recognises that they form a just basis for reconciliation.

It is precisely this combination of justice and forgiveness, and the opportunity for repentance it provides the wrong-doer, that is singled out for praise in the description of the saintly Irish King Brian (chapter 154):

> Brján konungr gaf upp útlogum sínum þrysvar ina somu sok; en ef þeir misgerðu optar, þá lét hann

dœma þá at lǫgum, ok má af þvílíku marka, hvílíkr
konungr hann var.

(King Brian would always forgive men he had
sentenced to outlawry, even when they committed the
same offence thrice; but if they transgressed yet again,
he lèt the law take its course. From this it can be
judged what kind of a king he was.)

Hrútr's example shows how the moment of
forgiveness and reconciliation marks the collapse of the
influence of the forces of darkness. We have space to look
at one last episode, which shows more about how the
operation of these forces is used as a powerful moral
metaphor. The episode, of interest here not least because it
has caused universal confusion among critics of *Njáls saga*,
concerns the case of Ámundi the Blind (chapter 106).
    This man is a Christian who has been blind from
birth. He appeals to God to help him get justice from his
father's killer, whereupon sight is miraculously given him
for just long enough to allow him to bury his axe in the
killer's head. It is obvious why critics have been uneasy at
this scene: since the Christians' God is the God of Love,
Whose commandment it is not to kill, it would appear that
at best the Christian author of *Njála* had a very inadequate
understanding of his God; at worst the scene can be read as
downright blasphemous.
    Seen against the background of the metaphor of
darkness and vision, however, the message of the episode is
clear and unambiguous. When Ámundi makes his appeal
to God, he sets out alternative courses of action: "enda
kann ek at segja þér, ef ek væra heileygr báðum augum, at
hafa skylda ek annathvárt fyrir fǫður minn fébœtr eða
mannhefndir, enda skipti guð með okkr!"
('And I can tell you this, that if my eyes were blest with sight,
I would get full compensation for my father or else take
blood-revenge. May God judge between us.')
    The miraculous granting of his sight gives Ámundi the
opportunity to seek justice by exercising one of his two
options: justice alone demands blood vengeance, while
justice combined with mercy would look for compensation.
It is Ámundi's tragedy that he fails to recognise that just as

God has shown him mercy in allowing him to see, the better, Christian course of action would be for him to allow his father's killer to live.

Ámundi's example contrasts with that of Hrútr. Whereas Hrútr escapes the power of the forces of darkness at the moment that he forgives his adversary, Ámundi plunges himself back into darkness with the downward stroke of his axe. The author of *Njáls saga* reveals his constant awareness of the interplay between metaphor and action in the bitter irony of the words Ámundi uses seconds before he takes his revenge: "Lofaðr sé guð, dróttinn minn! Sér nú, hvat hann vill." ('Praise be to the Lord my God. His will is now seen.')

The Supernatural in *Njáls saga*: a narratological approach

Rory McTurk
University of Leeds

In this paper[1] I shall use two types of specialised language (though neither, I hope, excessively) in discussing the supernatural in *Njáls saga*: on the one hand the language of narratology,[2] and on the other that of parapsychology.[3]

As for the former, I shall adopt the narratological distinction between *story* and *narrative*; the story is *what happens* (in this case in *Njáls saga*), whereas the narrative is *the statement of what happens*. The distinction may be clarified by reference to the order in which the events of the saga are brought to the reader's or listener's attention: whenever the narrative abandons the matter currently in hand to refer to past or future events, by the devices known as *analepsis* and *prolepsis* respectively, it is departing from the order in which events take place in the story. I shall also be using the narratological distinctions between *levels of narrative* and between *levels of focalisation*. The former distinction helps to answer the question of who is telling the story at a given moment, while the latter helps to determine who (if anyone) is witnessing its events at a given moment. To deal first with levels of narrative, it may be said that events narrated on the first level, or in the first degree, are those which the anonymous narrator of the saga reports directly; whereas events narrated on the second level (or in the second degree) are those reported in passages of direct speech by characters in the saga. As for levels of focalisation, events focalised in the first degree, or on the first level, are those which the narrator reports, without reference to witnesses, as having taken place; whereas events focalised in the second degree (or on the second level) are those which are stated to have been witnessed by characters in the saga — stated, that is, either by the characters themselves (in passages of direct speech) or by the anonymous narrator. This last consideration means that levels or degrees of focalisation do not always coincide with those of narrative, though they may often do so. Finally, I shall use the term *diegetic* to refer to events or characters that form part of the *diegesis* of *Njáls saga*, i.e. the world or universe in which its story, as narrated on the first level, takes place; and the term *metadiegetic*[4] for anyone or anything that forms part of the subject-matter of an account given in direct speech by one or another of the saga's characters, i.e. on the second level of narrative.

The language of parapsychology may be dealt with much more briefly. I shall use the terms *retrocognitive*, *telepathic*, and *precognitive* to refer to experiences in which characters in the saga receive notice, otherwise than by normal sensory communication, of events of the past, present, and future respectively. A retrocognitive dream, for example, is one that gives notice of a past event; a telepathic vision is one that gives notice of an event that takes place simultaneously with the vision itself; and a precognitive dream is one that gives notice of an event in the future.

References to *Njáls saga* in what follows are by chapter to the edition of Einar Ól. Sveinsson, 1954. Before proceeding to discuss and classify the supernatural incidents in *Njáls saga*, I should emphasise that I have not included among their number prophecies whose fulfilment may in my view be reasonably explained by reference to the human insight, natural wisdom, and worldly experience of those who make them; experience of the law is often involved here. Examples are Morðr gígja's words in Ch. 7 to his daughter Unnr about the procedure she must follow (and does follow, later in the same chapter) to get divorced from Hrútr Herjólfsson; Njáll's instructions to Gunnarr in Ch. 22 about how to recover Unnr's dowry from Hrútr (cf. chs. 23-24); Njáll's relatively general prophecies about the unhappiness of Gunnarr's marriage to Hallgerðr and the unexpected cause of his own death, in chs. 33 and 55 respectively; his more specific prophecy in Ch. 58 that many deaths will result from the horse-fight between the stallions belonging to Starkaðr Barkarson and Gunnarr (cf. Ch. 63); and Njáll's prophecy that Gunnarr's death will be caused by his (Gunnarr's) breaking the terms made in consequence of his slaying more than once in the same family, reported by Mǫrðr Valgarðsson to Þorgeirr Starkaðarson in Ch. 67 (cf. chs. 72, 75, and 77). Also in this category are jarl Hákon's prophecy at the end of Ch. 88 that the protection given by Þráinn Sigfússon to the trouble-maker Hrappr Ǫrgumleiðason (Víga-Hrappr) will lead to the deaths of both Þráinn and Hrappr (cf. Ch. 92); Njáll's prophecy in Ch. 94 that Þráinn's son Hǫskuldr, whom Njáll adopts as his foster-son after Þráinn's death, will grow up to be a good man — a prophecy fulfilled up to the moment of Hǫskuldr's slaying by Njáll's sons and Mǫrðr in Ch. 111; Njáll's forecast in Ch. 111 that the slaying of Hǫskuldr will lead to his own death and that of his wife and sons, though the career of his son-in-law, Kári Sǫlmundarson, will be attended by good luck (cf. chs. 128-30); Njáll's general statement in Ch. 120 that fate must take its course, made after Skarpheðinn's aggressive behaviour towards various chieftains at the Alþingi has called in question the amount of support Njáll and his sons will receive in attempting to reach a peaceful settlement with Flosi Þórðarson, the uncle of Hǫskuldr's wife Hildigunnr, over Hǫskuldr's slaying (cf. Ch. 123); and Gizurr (hvíti) Teitsson's accurate prediction, in Ch. 135, of Mǫrðr's initially negative response to Kári's request (made in the same chapter) that Mǫrðr should prosecute Flosi for the slaying of Njáll's son Helgi, who (in Ch. 129) had been killed by Flosi in trying to escape from the burning of Njáll and his family, led by Flosi and described in chs. 128-30. Mention may finally be made of Snorri goði Þorgrímsson's prediction in Ch. 139 that the two parties involved in this prosecution will come to blows at the Alþingi (cf. Ch. 145); and Eyjólfr Bǫlverksson's forecast in Ch. 144 (fulfilled in the same chapter) that Mǫrðr will bungle the prosecution.

   As will be clear from this list, predictions often occur in contexts of advice, and may be fulfilled if the advice, whether followed or not, turns out to have been well-founded. Actual words of advice, though, however well-chosen, are if anything even less worthy of consideration as partaking of the supernatural, in my view, than the prophecies just listed. Examples other than those already noted are Njáll's advice to Gunnarr, offered and taken in Ch. 56, to make terms with Otkell's relatives Gizurr hvíti and Geirr goði Ásgeirsson after the killing of Otkell by Gunnarr in Ch. 54; Njáll's legal advice to Gunnarr, offered in chs. 64-65 and carried into effect in Ch. 66, with the result that a settlement is reached between Gunnarr and the relatives of some of those he had slain after being ambushed by the brothers-in-law Starkaðr and Egill in Ch. 63; Mǫrðr's advice in Ch. 67 to Starkaðr's son Þorgeirr, which Þorgeirr carries out in chs. 68-72, to trap Gunnarr into killing Þorgeirr Otkelsson, so that Gunnarr, who has already killed Otkell, will then have killed twice in the same family, and be in danger of his life if he breaks the terms of the resulting settlement, as in fact he does in refusing to accept banishment in Ch. 75; Njáll's advice to his sons in Ch. 91 to give Þráinn a chance to make abusive comments at their expense before they kill him, so that they will not be open to the charge of killing without cause — advice which they follow, with humiliating results, before actually killing him in Ch. 92; Síðu-Hallr Þorsteinsson's advice to Flosi in Ch. 146, taken by Flosi in the next chapter, to make terms with Njáll's nephew, Þorgeirr skorargeirr Þórisson; and Síðu-Hallr's advice to Flosi in Ch. 147, acted on by him in Ch. 158 (the penultimate chapter of the saga), to go on a pilgrimage to Rome.

The supernatural incidents in *Njáls saga* may initially be divided into three categories, as follows: first, prophecies that come true (other than those already dealt with); the word 'prophecy' is here being used in a sense wide enough to include spells, and statements giving advance notice of the special properties of certain objects, such as Gunnarr's halberd (*atgeirr*)[5] and jarl Sigurðr's battle-standard (*merki*); secondly, retrocognitive, telepathic, and precognitive intimations, dreams, and visions; and thirdly, remarkable happenings for which no physical cause is apparent, and which are not covered by these first two categories.

In the first category there are two clear examples of spells: the one cast on Hrútr Herjólfsson by Queen Gunnhildr Qzurardóttir in Ch. 6 to prevent his finding sexual fulfilment with the woman to whom he is betrothed, followed in the same chapter by Hrútr's marriage to his betrothed, Unnr Marðardóttir, which is indeed sexually unfulfilled, and ends soon afterwards with their divorce (in Ch. 7); and the verse incantation in Ch. 12 in which Svanr, Hallgerðr's maternal uncle, who is protecting Þjóstólfr, Hallgerðr's foster-father and the slayer of her first husband, Þorvaldr Ósvífsson, successfully calls forth a fog to hinder Þorvaldr's father Ósvífr and his companions in their vengeful pursuit of Þjóstólfr. Both these spells are cast, by Gunnhildr and Svanr respectively, in passages of direct speech, i.e. on the second level of narrative, and the successful outcome of the spell is in each case narrated (and, as it happens, focalised also) on the first level (Ch. 6: *En fátt var með þeim Hrúti um samfarar...*,' But Hrútr and his wife could not enjoy normal conjugal relations'; Ch. 12:*...þá kom þoka mikil í móti þeim* 'then a thick fog came towards them'). They thus conform to what will emerge below as the normal pattern for prophecies in *Njáls saga*.

A less clear-cut case of a spell (in the sense of a prophecy that comes true) is that of Galdra-Heðinn's sacrifices in Ch. 101, the purpose of which is to bring about the death of the missionary Þangbrandr and his followers, but which succeed only in respect of Þangbrandr's horse, which disappears into the chasm that suddenly appears in its rider's path. The most impressively supernatural aspect of this incident, in my view, is Þangbrandr's miraculous escape, which belongs, and will be noted, in my third category of remarkable happenings below (p. 119f.) It may however be noted here that the sacrifices as well as the subsequent appearance of the chasm are narrated and focalised in the first degree, and that in this respect also the incident deviates from the normal pattern of prophecies in *Njáls saga*.

Next in this first category come the statements made by Tófi and Gunnarr in relation to Gunnarr's halberd, in chs. 30 and 72 respectively. These need to be discussed at some length, partly because the first of them is a somewhat doubtful example of supernatural events in this category, and partly because the halberd has an important unifying function in the saga's presentation of Gunnarr's career (in chs.19-99). When it first appears in Ch. 30, the halberd is in the possession of one Hallgrímr, a Viking encountered by Gunnarr on the Baltic island of Eysýsla. Tófi, who warns Gunnarr of Hallgrímr's hostile presence, explains that the halberd has the magical property of making a loud ringing noise as a portent of death through its agency. Gunnarr takes possession of the halberd after a fight with Hallgrímr in which Hallgrímr drops the halberd and Gunnarr kills him with it. The halberd is next mentioned in chs. 49-50, where Otkell Skarfsson, his brother Hallbjǫrn, and his friend Skamkell each refer to it briefly after Otkell has churlishly refused Gunnarr's handsome offers of compensation for the food stolen from Otkell at the instigation of Gunnarr's wife Hallgerðr. It is next referred to in Ch. 53, where Gunnarr, after being gashed by Otkell's spur as Otkell galloped past him while he was sowing, tells Skamkell, who was close by at the time, that he will see the halberd when next they meet. In Ch. 54, when Gunnarr is told at Hlíðarendi that Otkell is riding down along the river Markarfljót, he takes hold of the halberd, which rings loudly, and rides off; Gunnarr's mother Rannveig tells her son Kolskeggr of this incident, which Kolskeggr prophesies will have momentous consequences. Gunnarr catches up with Otkell, and kills him as well as Skamkell with the halberd. The weapon is next mentioned in Ch. 61, where Gunnarr takes it with him on his brief visit to Ásgrímr Elliða-Grímsson at Tunga; then in Ch. 62, where Gunnarr, on his way home from Tunga, speaks of just having had a dream in which he used the halberd to fight some wolves; and then again in Ch. 63, where the wolves of the dream turn out to have represented certain of Gunnarr's human enemies, who now attack him at Knafahólar, led by Starkaðr Barkarson and Egill Kolsson, and Gunnarr kills with the halberd both Egill and Starkaðr's son Bǫrkr. The halberd is next mentioned at the end of Ch. 71, only briefly, and then, much more dramatically, at the beginning of Ch. 72, where blood appears on it as Gunnarr and Kolskeggr are riding towards Rangá. Gunnarr, in a brief passage of direct speech, cites Ǫlvir as having said that such occurrences portended fierce encounters: "*ok sagði svá Ǫlvir bóndi, at þat væri fyrir stórfundum*", 'and Ǫlvir the farmer said that that should portend some great battle' (Ǫlvir was someone with whom Gunnarr had had dealings just before and after first acquiring the halberd, in chs. 29-31). Also in Ch. 72, Gunnarr is ambushed by Otkell's son Þorgeirr and others, and Gunnarr kills Þorgeirr and his kinsman Ǫnundr with the halberd. In Ch. 75, just before the famous scene in which Gunnarr decides to defy the three-year banishment from Iceland imposed on him by his settlement with Þorgeirr Otkelsson's relatives, it is said that Gunnarr, as he mounts his horse to leave Hlíðarendi, uses the halberd for vaulting into the saddle. In Ch. 77, when Gunnarr is attacked at Hlíðarendi by Þorgeirr's relatives and their followers, he slays with the halberd Þorgrímr Austmaðr and Þorbrandr Þorleiksson, and wounds with it Þorbrandr's brother Ásbrandr, before dying his heroic death. In Ch. 78 it is reported that Gunnarr's mother Rannveig would not allow the halberd to be buried with him and would only let it be touched by Gunnarr's prospective avenger. In the next chapter, 79, Gunnarr's son Hǫgni takes down the halberd, which then rings loudly (*Hǫgni tekr ofan atgeirinn, ok sǫng í honum*). Egged on by Rannveig, he avenges his father with the help of Njáll's son Skarpheðinn, killing with the halberd Hróaldr Geirsson and Þorgeirr Starkaðarson, who had boasted of their share in Gunnarr's slaying.

Thus, after its acquisition by Gunnarr, the halberd kills on five separate occasions, but only on the first and last of these (the killing of Otkell and Skamkell and that of Hróaldr and Þorgeirr) does it make the ringing noise it is supposed to make according to Tófi's prophecy (in the sense of the word explained above, p. 105). On both these occasions, moreover, the noise occurs just after the halberd has been grasped by the prospective killer — Gunnarr himself in the former case, and his son Hǫgni in the latter. It is perhaps not surprising that a halberd should ring when grasped by someone intent on killing with it, and this raises the question of whether it is making the noise in fulfilment of the prophecy, or simply because it has been energetically grasped. Is the ringing of the halberd on these occasions an example of the supernatural, or not? There would be less doubt on this point if the halberd had been presented as ringing of its own accord, without first being touched. The second occasion when the halberd kills (the killing of Egill and Bǫrkr) is, it is true, evoked in advance by Gunnarr's dream of the wolves, in which the halberd figures; but this dream, which belongs in the second of my three main categories of supernatural incidents rather than here, does not conform to the expectations raised by Tófi's prophecy, and does not, indeed, relate specifically to the halberd, though Gunnarr, in his account of the dream, briefly mentions it. The fourth occasion when the halberd kills (Gunnarr's last stand, when he slays Þorgrímr and Þorbrandr) is not, as far as I can see, specifically portended by any supernatural event; but the third, the killing of Þorgeirr Otkelsson and Ǫnundr, is dramatically preceded by the appearance of blood on the halberd. This, again, is not what Tófi's prophecy had led us to expect; but when it happens Gunnarr, as already shown, quotes Ǫlvir as saying that such an occurrence portended fierce encounters. In narratological terms, this statement of Gunnarr's is an example of *completing internal analepsis*, analepsis being, as already indicated (p. 102), an evocation of an earlier event. It is 'completing' (rather than 'repeating') because the event evoked (Ǫlvir's explanation of the portent) has not in fact been mentioned earlier in the narrative — this is the first we hear of it; and it is 'internal' (rather than 'external') because this event, though it has not been mentioned until now, must be assumed to have taken place within the period of time covered by the narrative so far, rather than outside (i.e. prior to) that period (cf. Genette 1980, 48-67); it presumably happened at some stage of Gunnarr's dealings with Ǫlvir, described in chs. 29 and 31.

The actual appearance of blood on the halberd belongs, of course, in my third category of supernatural incidents (remarkable happenings not covered by the first two categories) and will be noted in the appropriate place below. Here I would very tentatively suggest that the author of *Njáls saga* felt, as I do, that in describing the halberd's ringing noise he had left rather too much doubt in the minds of his audience as to whether this was happening by accident or as a result of Tófi's prophecy, and that he added the motif of blood appearing on the halberd in order to make it quite clear that supernatural forces were at work in connection with it. I would argue that the appearance of blood on the halberd differs from the prophecy it occasions and from other prophecies here under consideration in being a supernatural event in its own right, irrespective of the prophecy and of whether or not it is fulfilled; it might even be argued that it is more supernatural than the kind of event that typically constitutes a prophecy in *Njáls saga*. In this saga a prophecy usually operates on two levels of narrative: the *metadiegetic*, where the events are evoked in direct speech by one of the characters, and the *diegetic*, where the events prophesied take place within the diegesis, or the universe of the story proper, as the narrator tells it. If it is accepted that a prophecy must be fulfilled in order to qualify as a supernatural incident, then it may be maintained that, except in the relatively rare cases where prophecies are made in indirect speech, a prophecy in *Njáls saga* is supernatural only insofar as it operates on both the metadiegetic and the diegetic levels. Neither the prophetic statement nor the event that bears it out would normally count, on its own, as supernatural; it is only when the one is seen in relation to the other that either may be recognised as such. By contrast, the appearance of blood on Gunnarr's halberd is a purely diegetic event which does not require reference to any other level of narrative for confirmation of its supernatural character. It is narrated in the first rather than the second degree, i.e. by the narrator rather than by any of the characters, which suggests that the narrator is taking relatively full responsibility for his account of the occurrence, as also does the fact that the event is not only narrated, but also focalised, in the first degree; that is, it is presented as having actually happened (irrespective of whether or not witnesses were present), rather than as merely having been perceived to happen (by one or more of the characters); it is as though the narrator, as well as the witnesses present at this point in the story, saw it take place. Focaliser and narrator, then, are here one and the same; but it should be re-emphasised that this is not always so, and that levels or degrees of focalisation do not always coincide with those of narrative.

Second-degree focalisation, or focalisation through a character, may often occur in conjunction with first-degree narrative, i.e. on the diegetic level, and when it does so, it does not make the events focalised any less diegetic. It does, however, imply a greater distance from the narrator (here viewed as a focaliser) than is implied by focalisation in the first degree, just as second-degree narrative implies a greater distance from the narrator (here viewed as a reporter of events) than is implied by first-degree narrative (cf. Bal 1977, 115-27). These points may be illustrated by contrasting the appearance of blood on the halberd with the chanting of verses by Gunnarr's ghost in his burial-mound, of which two accounts are given in Ch. 78. Here the ghost's activities are diegetic, i.e. they are narrated in the first degree, but they are at the same time focalised in the second degree; each account is introduced by an expression meaning, 'it seemed to them', (*þeim þótti, þeim sýndisk*), and is presented in terms of what was witnessed by observers — a shepherd and a housemaid in the first case, and, in the second, Njáll's son Skarpheðinn and Gunnarr's son Hǫgni. In the second account in particular the narrator seems at pains to disclaim full responsibility for the report he gives, using in addition to *þeim sýndisk* such expressions as *þeir þóttusk ...sjá* and *þeir sá* ('they thought they saw', 'they saw'). This event, which also belongs in my third main category of supernatural incidents, will be noted below (p. 120).

The appearance of blood on the halberd and the prophecy occasioned by it are closely parallelled by the sequence of events in Ch. 156 of *Njáls saga*, where the Viking Bróðir, an apostate Christian who subsequently takes part in the Battle of Clontarf, is subjected together with his followers, shortly before the battle, to supernatural harassment on three successive nights: by rain in the form of boiling blood on the first, by weapons fighting of their own accord on the second, and by ravens with iron-like beaks and talons on the third. These events, like the appearance of blood on Gunnarr's halberd, are narrated and focalised in the first degree. Bróðir consults with his sworn brother Óspakr, who explains in direct speech (much as Gunnarr explains the significance of blood on the halberd) that the blood-rain portends bloodshed, the weapons battle, and the ravens the demons that will receive Bróðir and his followers into hell. This prophecy is fulfilled in the following chapter at the Battle of Clontarf, where Bróðir and his men are all slain by the Irish and their allies, but not before Bróðir has slain the Irish king Brján, an event immediately preceded in the narrative by an account of how Hrafn inn rauði, another of the king's opponents, sees while swimming a river a vision of demons attempting to drag him down to hell. These events are all narrated, if not at all stages focalised, in the first degree. Thus the prophecy itself resembles the one relating to blood on the halberd, not only in conforming to the normal pattern of emergence on the metadiegetic level and fulfilment on the diegetic, but also in a relatively exceptional way, insofar as it is occasioned by a diegetic supernatural occurrence focalised in the first degree.

Other examples of the supernatural in the category of prophecies are, of course, Sæunn's prophecy in Ch. 124, fulfilled in Ch. 129, that a pile of chickweed (*arfasáta*) behind the farm at Bergþórshváll will be used for kindling in the burning of Njáll and Bergþóra; Bergþóra's prophecy in Ch. 127, just before the burning, that the meal she is preparing will be the last she ever serves to her household; the Viking Bróðir's information, obtained by witchcraft in Ch. 157 and shown to be accurate later in the chapter, that if the Scandinavians join battle with the Irish on Good Friday, the Irish king Brján will win the battle, but lose his life; and, in the same chapter, Ámundi hvíti's information, evidently based on what he has seen so far of the Battle of

Clontarf, that everyone who carries jarl Sigurðr's battle-standard gets killed; this is then confirmed in the case of Sigurðr himself, who takes the standard and attempts to conceal it on his person, but is slain soon afterwards.

Apart from the ambiguous case of Galdra-Heðinn's sacrifices, already discussed (p. 106), Bróðir's information about the outcome of the Battle of Clontarf is as far as I can see the only supernatural prophecy in *Njáls saga* that is not made at least partly in direct speech; it is thus exceptional in being exclusively diegetic. It may however be noted that the prophecy itself, which consists in the information obtained by Bróðir by magical means, and narrated in indirect speech, is focalised (by Bróðir himself) in the second degree.

Moving on to my second category of supernatural incidents, I apply the terms *retrocognitive, telepathic,* and *precognitive,* as already explained (p. 103), to experiences in which people receive notice of past, present and future events respectively, without first having the information that would make it possible to infer their occurrence. These experiences most often take the form of dreams or visions, though occasionally they involve accesses of insight perhaps best described as 'intimations'.

It is sometimes hard to say for certain whether an incident is retrocognitive, telepathic, or precognitive, but as far as I can see the only clear-cut instance of retrocognition in *Njáls saga* is Hǫskuldr Dala-Kollsson's dream in which, as he relates it in Ch. 23, a large bear leaves Hǫskuldr's homestead with two bear-cubs and goes to the home of Hǫskuldr's half-brother Hrútr Herjólfsson. Discussing the dream with his household, Hǫskuldr concludes that the bear is the fetch (*fylgja*) of Gunnarr of Hlíðarendi, and then realises that it was Gunnarr who had visited him in disguise with two companions and stayed at his home over the night previous to that on which he had the dream. Hǫskuldr now visits Hrútr, and discovers that Gunnarr had gone from his home to Hrútr's, still in disguise, and had found out from Hrútr how to reopen legal proceedings as a result of which Hrútr would have to repay his divorced wife's dowry; he had then left Hrútr's home during the night of Hǫskuldr's dream. The effectiveness of Gunnarr's stratagem, which he had carried out on Njáll's advice, given in Ch. 22, is seen in Ch. 24, where Hrútr is forced to pay up.

As for telepathic incidents, an obvious example is Svanr's sudden realisation in Ch. 12 that Ósvífr and his followers are on their way to attack him and Þjóstólfr in the circumstances described above (p. 106); he yawns, as it was believed people did when their enemies, intentions towards them were hovering near them in spirit form (see Einar Ól. Sveinsson 1954, 37, n.7), and states that Ósvífr's fetches (*fylgjur*) are attacking him and Þjóstólfr just as Ósvífr and his followers are entering Bjarnarfjǫrðr, where Svanr and Þjóstólfr are at the time. Another example, also involving fetches, occurs in Ch. 69, where Þorgeirr Starkaðarson and Þorgeirr Otkelsson, on their way to attack Gunnarr at Hlíðarendi, enter a wood with their twenty-two followers, are overcome by drowsiness, and fall asleep. Njáll, however, who is spending the night at Þórólfsfell, east of Hlíðarendi, cannot sleep, because, as he explains, he can see the "fierce-looking fetches" (*fylgjur grimmligar*) of Gunnarr's enemies, though he also notes that they are behaving without purpose (*ráðlausliga*). Soon afterwards he hears from a shepherd of the twenty-four men asleep in the wood, and realizes what is afoot; he sends a warning message to Gunnarr and seeks out the two Þorgeirrs, scaring them off with comments contrasting their carelessness with Gunnarr's vigilance and general formidableness. Njáll is not able to avert catastrophe for long, however; in chs. 71-72 the two Þorgeirrs, encouraged by Mǫrðr Valgarðsson, ambush Gunnarr with the results indicated above in the discussion of Gunnarr's halberd. A third instance occurs in Ch. 85, where Helgi Njálsson, after being taken by Kári Sǫlmundarson to the court of jarl Sigurðr of the Orkneys following the help given by Kári to Helgi and his brother Grímr in a battle against some Vikings elsewhere in the British Isles, falls silent as time goes on, and, when the jarl asks him the reason, indicates that territories of the jarl's in Scotland have been severely threatened by hostile action on the part of the Scots — information which turns out to be accurate in this and the following chapter, and which Kári accounts for, interestingly enough, by reference to the fact that Helgi's father, Njáll, is prescient (*forspár*). A fourth example, rather less convincing than the one just given, is provided in Ch. 88, where jarl Hákon, anxious to be avenged on Víga-Hrappr for desecrating a pagan sanctuary, discovers Hrappr's whereabouts as a result of spending some time alone on his knees with his hands over his eyes. He does not catch Hrappr, however, who runs too fast for him; and when Hrappr subsequently takes refuge on board Þráinn Sigfússon's ship, which is just about to return to Iceland from Norway, the jarl searches the ship three times, but does not find Hrappr, who is hiding in a different place each time. After the second of his three searches the jarl acknowledges that his telepathic powers seem to work when he is ashore, but fail him when he is on board ship. It may be noted that, insofar as it provides an example of a telepathic incident, the saga's account of these events has no metadiegetic element; it certainly includes passages of direct speech, some of them spoken by jarl Hákon, but none of them is used to report or explain the jarl's strange methods for detecting Hrappr's whereabouts, which are narrated (and focalised) in the first degree. A fifth example, even less striking than the fourth, though different from it in functioning in the normal way on both the metadiegetic and diegetic levels, is found at the beginning of Ch. 112, where Hildigunnr wakes up on the morning on which Hǫskuldr has been killed (as described in Ch. 111), notices his absence, says she has had evil dreams, and orders a search to be made for him; soon afterwards she herself finds the body. It is reasonable to suppose that she had the dreams at much the same time as the killing took place.

It seems fair to include in the sub-category of telepathic incidents as here defined five at least of the six marvellous occurrences described just after the account of the Battle of Clontarf in Ch. 157; there seems little doubt that all six of them are supposed to take place contemporaneously with the battle, rather than before or after it (see Einar Ól. Sveinsson 1954, 454, n.1; 459, n.2). The relevant part of the chapter describes how news of the battle is made known by supernatural means, in varying degrees of accuracy and detail, in different parts of the British Isles and Iceland, and in the Faroes. All six occurrences are to be regarded for present purposes as diegetic, in that they are narrated in the first degree; the fact that the first and last of them include verses spoken by characters, the content of which must therefore be seen as metadiegetic, is irrelevant here. Only the third, the appearance of blood on the priest's chasuble at Svínafell in Iceland, on Good Friday, the day of the battle, so that he has to take the garment off, is focalised as well as narrated in the first degree. Since this means that, as the saga describes it, the occurrence in question gives very little sense of news of the battle being communicated to a particular person, I have chosen not to regard it as a telepathic incident, and to reserve it for inclusion in my third and final category of supernatural incidents, to be discussed below (p. 119ff.) The remaining five occurrences, however, which I number here according to their placing in the six-part sequence, are all focalised in the second degree; the first and fourth of them, I would further note, are, like the third, stated to have taken place on Good Friday. The first is focalised by a certain Dǫrruðr, who, looking through the window of a woman's bower in Caithness, sees some women working at a loom which has human heads as weights, human intestines as weft and warp, a sword as beater and an arrow as shuttle, and chanting the verses now known as *Darraðarljóð*, in which the women present themselves as valkyries, and sing of the deaths of a king and a jarl, and of the lasting grief of the Irish. The second occurrence, evidently of the same kind as the first (*slíkr atburðr*) is focalised by a certain Brandr Gneistason, who witnesses it in the Faroe Islands; the fourth by the priest at Þváttá in Iceland, to whom there appears (*sýndisk*) a deep sea full of terrors by the altar of his church, so that his singing of the office is delayed; the fifth by one Hárekr, who, in the Orkneys, thinks he sees (*þóttisk sjá*) jarl Sigurðr and some of his followers riding behind a hill, never to be seen again; and the sixth, finally, by jarl Gilli, who has a dream in the Hebrides in which a man called Herfiðr appears to him, says he has come from Ireland, and then tells him in a *dróttkvætt* strophe of a battle in Ireland at which jarl Sigurðr died, and King Brjánn, though victorious, died also.

The precognitive incidents in *Njáls saga*, which form a third sub-category within the second category of supernatural incidents here under consideration, must now be glanced at. The first obvious example is Gunnarr's dream of the wolves, experienced and described by him in Ch. 62; this dream, and its fulfilment in the following chapter, have already been discussed in connection with Gunnarr's halberd (p. 107). The second example of precognition occurs in Ch. 81, where Gunnarr's brother Kolskeggr dreams (in Denmark) that a man radiant with light asks him in direct speech to follow him, saying that he will find him a bride, and that Kolskeggr will be his knight. Kolskeggr agrees to this in the dream, and on waking consults a wise man who in narratised (or indirect) speech interprets the dream as meaning that Kolskeggr will go to southern lands and become a knight of God. The dream appears to be fulfilled at the end of the chapter, where it is reported that, after being baptised in Denmark, Kolskeggr went by way of Russia to Constantinople, where he married and rose to a high rank in the Varangian guard. This incident differs from the normal pattern of incidents in this category in that the dream is narrated in the first degree (i.e. by the narrator) rather than in the second (i.e. by the character who has had the dream); it is however focalised in the second degree (i.e. by the dreamer). While it is thus primarily diegetic, the passage of direct speech in which the dream-figure foretells Kolskeggr's future does provide it with a metadiegetic, or second-degree narrative, element, and the incident in fact follows the normal pattern of a supernatural prophecy in *Njáls saga*, with the difference that the prophecy's metadiegetic element here occurs as part of a dream, focalised in the second degree. Much the same may be said of the third example, Hildiglúmr Runólfsson's vision of the *gandreið*, or witch-ride, recorded in Ch. 125. The only difference between this and the second example

in narratological terms is that here it is not just the person
encountered in the vision, but also the person consulted
afterwards about its meaning, who speaks in direct rather
than narratised speech. Hildiglúmr looks towards the west
from his home at Reykir in Skeið on a Sunday night twelve
weeks before winter and thinks he sees (*þóttisk hann sjá*) a
man on a grey horse within a circle of fire. The man, who
appears to be (*sýndisk*) as black as pitch, rides close by
Hildiglúmr holding a blazing firebrand in his hand and
reciting (in direct speech) a verse-passage in *fornyrðislag* in
which he describes his horse as a bringer of ill-luck (*ills
valdandi*), and compares Flosi's plans to a firebrand
speeding through the air. He then seems to Hildiglúmr (*þá
þótti honum hann*) to fling the firebrand eastwards towards
the mountains, causing a vast fire to flare up. On his
father's advice, Hildiglúmr reports the vision to Hjalti
Skeggjason, who tells him that what he has seen is a witch-
ride, which always portends disaster (here, of course, it
portends the burning of Njáll, led by Flosi, which is
described in the next five chapters). Hjalti's statement in
direct speech and its subsequent confirmation conform to
the normal pattern of a supernatural prophecy, except that
the prophecy is here occasioned by a vision focalised in the
second degree; in other respects the incident is exactly
parallel to the one taken as the last example, as already
indicated.

The remaining three examples all operate in the
normal way on the metadiegetic and diegetic levels. The
next one, the fourth, is Njáll's statement in Ch. 127, just
after his wife Bergþóra has served food to their household
for what she prophesies is the last time, that he thinks he
can see all parts of the room in which they are sitting, that
both the gable-walls appear to have collapsed, and that
there seems to be blood on the table and the food. Here he
is clearly having a precognitive intimation of the destruction
and death caused by the burning, and described in chs. 129-
30. The fifth example occurs in Ch. 133, where, shortly
after the burning, Flosi tells Ketill of Mǫrk of a dream he
has just had at Svínafell of how the Lómagnúpr cliff had
opened to let out a man dressed in a goatskin, carrying an

iron staff, and calling out a number of people's names. Of those named whom Flosi himself specifies in his account of the dream, all except one had supported him either at the burning or in the feud leading up to it; the one exception, Eyjólfr Bǫlverksson, later gives him his support (chs. 138–45) in connection with the prosecution against him at the Alþingi for the slaying of Njáll's son Helgi at the burning. The man had given his name as Járngrímr and was on his way to the Alþingi, where a battle was to take place in which (so he claimed in a *dróttkvætt*-strophe) a mighty warrior would emerge. Ketill interprets the dream as meaning that all those called are doomed to die; and all those specified by Flosi are in fact subsequently killed, most of them by Kári, either in the fight that breaks out at the Alþingi in Ch. 145 or on various subsequent occasions. The sixth and final example occurs in Ch. 134, where Yngvildr Þorkelsdóttir, asked why she is weeping just after her sons Þorkell and Þorvaldr have agreed to give Flosi their support at the Alþingi, says she has dreamt that Þorvaldr was wearing a red tunic that seemed to fit him as tightly as if he had been sewn into it, and red leggings similarly tightly bound. She was distressed to see that he was so uncomfortable, but could do nothing to help him. That this is a precognitive intimation of Þorvaldr's death may be concluded from Ch. 145, where he is killed by Þorgeirr skorargeirr Þórisson in the fight at the Alþingi.

With only a few exceptions, then, the incidents in these first two categories operate on both the metadiegetic and diegetic levels, and are supernatural only insofar as they operate on both. Furthermore, while the diegetic element in each of them is usually essential to the story, the metadiegetic element is not. This implies that the author of the saga is interested in them not so much because they are supernatural as because they are useful proleptic (or in some cases analeptic) devices.

The incidents in the third category, now to be discussed, are, by contrast, almost exclusively diegetic, in that they are narrated predominantly in the first degree, and may in general be recognised as supernatural without reference to any other level or degree of narrative; what metadiegetic elements they have are in each case subordinate to the diegetic element. Some of them, however, are focalised in the second degree, which presumably means that from the point of view of the narrator (if not the author) the incidents so focalised are less certainly supernatural than those focalised (as well as narrated) in the first. The incidents focalised in the second degree may be listed as follows: Gunnarr's ghost, twice witnessed in Ch. 78, and discussed above (p. 111); the verses heard among the flames at Bergþórshváll after the burning, in Ch. 130; the marks found on Skarpheðinn's body after the burning, in Ch. 132; and Hrafn inn rauði's vision of hell at the Battle of Clontarf in Ch. 157, noted above (p. 112). Those focalised as well as narrated in the first degree may be listed as follows: the appearance of blood on Gunnarr's halberd in Ch. 72, discussed above (p. 106-11); Þangbrandr's miraculous escape from Galdra-Heðinn's sorcery in Ch. 101 (referred to above, p. 106); Þangbrandr's defeat of the berserk Ótryggr by miraculous means in Ch. 103; Ámundi the Blind's temporary gift of sight, enabling him to kill Lýtingr, in Ch. 106; Þorkell hákr's slaying of fabulous monsters on the continent, reported in Ch. 119; the unburnt state of Njáll's and Bergþóra's bodies after the burning, in Ch. 132, and, in the same chapter, the continuous spouting of blood from Þórhallr Ásgrímsson's ears when he hears of Njáll's death; the gigantic waves which cause Flosi to land in the Orkneys in Ch. 153; Bróðir's three-night harassment in Ch. 156, discussed above (pp. 111-2); Bróðir's invulnerability at the Battle of Clontarf and his long delay in dying at the hands of his captors, in Ch. 157, and, in the same chapter, the healing quality of King Brjánn's blood and the miraculous grafting of his head to his body; and, finally, the portent on Good Friday at Svínafell in Iceland, also in Ch. 157, and discussed above (p. 116).

It will be noticed that most of the incidents in the second of these two lists take place in connection with the conversion of Iceland, the burning of Njáll, and the Battle of Clontarf, all events of greater or lesser Christian significance in *Njáls saga* (cf. Schach 1984, 120-22; Maxwell 1957-61, 35-46; Fox 1963, 301-09). The only exceptions are the blood on Gunnarr's halberd, Þorkell hákr's monster-slayings, and the gigantic waves. The first of these is included in the saga for special reasons, as I have argued above (p. 110); the second may be explained away as a completing internal analepsis of the kind known as heterodiegetic, its purpose being to introduce Þorkell hákr by dwelling on his antecedents (cf. Genette 1980, 50); and the third is too minor to disturb the general impression given by the list, which is that the author of *Njáls saga* wishes to draw special attention to the incidents in question, and to the decidedly Christian contexts in which they mostly occur, by emphasising their supernatural character. The fact that they are narrated on the first level as well as focalised in the first degree strongly suggests that the author wishes them to be regarded as more unambiguously supernatural than any of the other incidents considered here. This argument, if accepted, may be used in support of a view for which other students of *Njáls saga* have produced other arguments: that the conversion of Iceland is thematically as well as structurally central in the story of *Njáls saga* (cf. Schach 1984, 120-22; Maxwell 1957-61, 35-46; Fox 1963, 301-09; Lönnroth 1975, 69-73).

Elsewhere, in a discussion of *Eyrbyggja saga* (McTurk 1987), I have distinguished between subjectivist and objectivist approaches to the supernatural by creative writers. Subjectivist statements, at their simplest, are characterised by second-degree focalisation in combination with either first- or second-level narrative; whereas objectivist statements are characterised by first-degree focalisation in combination with (inevitably) first-level narrative. In accounts of supernatural experiences, subjectivist statements tend to imply that supernatural phenomena exist only in the minds of those who experience them, whereas objectivist statements tend to imply that such phenomena exist independently of those who experience them. What has emerged from the present study, I believe, is that in *Njáls saga*, where the supernatural is concerned, objectivist statements are for the most part reserved for accounts of supernatural events of specifically Christian significance. I would finally emphasise that a subjectivist or objectivist statement in Old Icelandic will not necessarily survive as such in a translation, and that anyone wishing to check the points made here should of course do so by reference to the Old Icelandic text. If indeed the present study achieves nothing more than to direct or redirect readers of *Njáls saga* from translations to the original, it will at least have achieved something.

Bibliography and Abbreviations

Bal, M. 1977. "Narration et focalisation: pour une théorie des instances du récit". *Poétique* 29, 107-27.

Bal, M. 1985. *Narratology. Introduction to the theory of narrative.* (tr. Christine van Boheemen).

Bayerschmidt, C.F. and Hollander, L.M. (tr.) 1955. *Njál's Saga.*

Cleasby, R. and Vigfússon, G. 1957. *An Icelandic-English Dictionary.*

Ebon, M. (ed.) 1978. *The Signet handbook of parapsychology.*

Fox, D. 1963. "Njáls saga and the Western literary tradition". *Comparative Literature* 15, 289-310.

Genette, G. 1980. *Narrative Discourse.* (tr. Jane E. Lewin).

Genette, G. 1988. *Narrative Discourse Revisited.* (tr. Jane E. Lewin).

Heywood, R. 1978. *The Sixth Sense. An enquiry into extra-sensory perception.*

Lindow, J. 1986. "*Þorsteins þáttr skelks* and the verisimilitude of supernatural experience in saga literature". In Lindow, J., Lönnroth, L. and Weber, G.W. (eds.) *Structure and meaning in Old Norse Literature. New approaches to textual analysis and literary criticism,* 264-80.

Lönnroth, L. 1975. "Structural divisions in the Njála manuscripts". *Arkiv för nordisk filologi* 90, 49-79.

Magnusson, M. and Pálsson, H. (tr.) 1960. *Njál's Saga*

Maxwell, I.R. 1957-61. "Pattern in Njáls saga". *Saga-Book* 15, 17-47.

McTurk, R. 1987. "The treatment of the supernatural in saga-narrative". In Allan, R.D.S. and Barnes, M.P. (eds.) *Proceedings of the Seventh Biennial Conference of Teachers of Scandinavian Studies in Great Britain and Northern Ireland, held at University College London, March 23-25, 1987,* 191-206.

Schach, P. 1984. *Icelandic sagas.*

SISC: The Sixth International Saga Conference 28.7-2.8.1985. Workshop papers.

Sveinsson, E. Ól. (ed.) 1954. *Brennu-Njáls saga.*

---

1   An earlier version of this paper was delivered at the Sixth International Saga Conference held at Helsingør in 1985; a brief summary of that version appears in the Workshop Papers of the Conference, *SISC,* II (1985, 775). The paper was later delivered in revised form at the Viking Society Student Conference on *Njáls saga* held at Birkbeck College, London, on March 3, 1990, and the present version, which follows that revised one closely, has also appeared in *Saga-Book* 23 (1990), 28-45. While the revisions do not include a discussion of Lindow 1986, which has appeared since this paper was first delivered and is reviewed by Andrew Wawn in *Saga-Book* 22 (1988), 299, I strongly recommend it for purposes of comparison and contrast with the approach adopted here.   I am grateful to the editors of the *Saga-Book*, particularly Desmond Slay, for a number of very helpful suggestions of which I have done my best to take account in the present, final version of the paper.

2   Here I am basing myself on Genette 1980 and 1988, and also, though to a lesser extent, on Bal 1977 and 1985.

3   Here I have made use of the Glossary of Terms in Ebon 1978, 509-12, and of Heywood 1978, 17.

4   I am sufficiently persuaded by Genette's defence (1988, 91-95) of his earlier use (1980, 231-37) of the term *metadiegetic* to adopt it here in preference to the term *hypodiegetic,* which I have used elsewhere (SISC, II, 1985, 775, and McTurk 1987) in discussing the supernatural in Icelandic literature.

5   I have borrowed the term *halberd* here, *faute de mieux*, from Cleasby-Vigfusson 1957 (where it appears under *atgeirr*). Bayerschmidt-Hollander 1955 and Magnusson-Pálsson 1960 also use it in their translations of *Njáls saga*.

Vikings and Celts

Peter Robinson
Oxford University

For over two hundred years, from around 820 to 1040 AD, the Viking and Celtic worlds were in full collision. Vivid episodes in *Njáls saga* and in *Laxdœla saga* tell how Vikings and Celts fought, traded, even loved, through the lands "vestan um haf": Ireland, Scotland and the islands. Beside the historical evidence of widespread and long contact between the two peoples a glance at their literatures shows striking affinities. Both affected fiendishly difficult poetry; both enjoyed long prose narratives in the vernacular interspersed with poetry, a form apparently found nowhere else in Europe at the time.

One might expect, then, a flourishing scholarly literature tracing the passage of influences between the Viking and Celtic worlds. Yet one can now read whole books about Old Norse literature, on the sagas or the poetry, that have nothing at all to say about the question of possible Celtic influence on their particular corner of Old Norse. In the index of the latest bibliography of Old Norse Literature under "foreign influences and parallels" there are eight references to discussion of "Celtic", in some 350 pages of text, against sixteen English, fourteen for Latin, and even five for African and five for Asian (Clover and Lindow 1985, 384-5). The subject is too hard. Or it is irrelevant. Or there is no way of determining what is common inheritance from our Indo-European forbears, what direct influence. Voices saying "there is something just like this in the *Mabinogion*, or in the *Táin*, or in a modern Gaelic folktale" are best ignored.

Influence across linguistic and cultural barriers is indeed notoriously difficult to prove. But the attempt is worth making. Here is an Irish account of the Viking invasions of Ireland, written around 1100 or earlier and describing the Danish assault on Munster around 920. This is how one Irishman saw the Vikings:

> "The whole of Munster was plundered by them and devastated...There was no place in Erinn without

numerous fleets of Danes and pirates ... they ravaged
the estates of the chieftains, and the churches, and the
sanctuaries. This furious, ferocious, pagan, ruthless,
wrathful people felt neither veneration nor honour for
God or man. They killed the kings and the chieftains,
the brave and the valiant, the stout knights,
champions, young lords, and the greater part of all the
heroes and warriors. They carried off the blooming
lively women, the modest mild comely maidens, and
the pleasant, stately, blue-eyed young women, the
gentle well-brought up youths — all these they carried
off into oppression and bondage over the broad green
sea."

(Todd 1867, 41-3)

For some 200 years, according to this rather lurid
account, the Vikings stormed over Ireland. A Viking queen,
one Ota, even seated herself on the high altar of
Clonmacnois and there carried out pagan divination (Todd
1867, 13). Nor do we have to rely exclusively on tabloid
history such as this. Archaeology, the sagas, evidence of
Irish borrowings from Norse, all confirm a large Viking
presence in Ireland between around 820 and 1040 AD (Ó
Cuív 1962). In the Western Isles, in Scotland, in Orkney, in
Shetland, Norseman lived beside Celt for centuries after
that.

Despite the popular image, it was not all blood.
Certainly the Vikings came as invaders, but as they stayed
they became more like peacable settlers — "a domestic
factor in the life of Ireland", as one scholar puts it (E.
MacNeill, quoted in Chadwick 1962, 34). Especially, the
Vikings gave Ireland commerce. The first coinage struck in
Ireland was issued by the Norse kingdom of Dublin. The
basic Irish vocabulary for commerce is borrowed from Old
Norse, e.g. the words for market, penny and others. Many of
the words associated with sailing in Irish come from Norse.
Many names of coastal places in some parts of Wales
likewise come from Old Norse: for example Anglesea,
Fishguard, Swansea and Ramsey (Richards 1962, 55-7). The
fortified sea-bases established as trading centres by the
Vikings became the towns and cities of modern Ireland.
According to the annals, Dublin itself was founded by
Vikings on a ford of the river Liffey in 841.

Celt and Viking lived side by side for centuries, and Celt learnt business from Viking. What did Viking learn from Celt? For the first scholars to look at this question, notably the great Norwegian philologist Sophus Bugge, the answer was simple. All Old Norse literature — the Eddic poetry, the family sagas, the skaldic poetry — grew from Celtic roots. Bugge argued this in a flood of books and articles (for example his *The Home of the Eddic Poems*, tr. Schofield 1899) with an erudition that is startling and occasionally frightening. It is very easy to ridicule Bugge's arguments. Taking them to their logical extreme, the Vikings appear an amazing mixture of rapists and scholars. They would take time off from a summer's pillaging for a day-trip to look at the Bewcastle Cross, or run into the monastic library to read the latest Irish translation of Meleager (Bugge 1899, 10-11; 97-8.) Thus, the reaction against Bugge has been so complete that many scholars just will not look at questions of borrowing from Celtic at all. Or, what is much the same, nothing short of an affidavit from the author, "I x borrowed this motif a from b and put it in my story c", will satisfy their need for proof (cf. Sims-Williams 1982a, 1982b).

One modern answer to the question of what Viking learnt from Celt is, simply, nothing. As one scholar, the expert on Irish and Scandinavian folk-tales Reidar Christiansen, puts it: "no Irish story — not even the name of an Irish hero — has been found in northern tradition, and of other Irish elements, such as loan words, the number is strictly limited" (Christiansen 1959, 225). Further, there is a plausible explanation for this apparent failure. That is the Old Irish language itself. To quote Kenneth Jackson: "Old Irish was a language of such unbelievable grammatical complication that it is difficult to see how anybody could have spoken it" (Jackson 1962, 7). If the Irish had such difficulty with their own language that they had to replace it with early Modern Irish, one can reasonably presume that the Vikings had no hope of learning it. The theory is that the Vikings learnt nothing because they could not even talk to the Celts.

The picture of a Viking tradition completely innocent of Celtic influence can not stand. Over the last century a

succession of scholars have pointed out a mass of individual
instances of Celtic influence in Viking tradition. Firstly,
there are loan-words. Indeed, there are relatively few such,
but some have a significance beyond their number. The
title of the Eddic poem *Rígsþula* is based on the Irish word
for king; and the poem leads up to the birth of a king: the
poem contains several other motifs with strong Celtic
analogues. One could also point to *gjalt*, from Irish *geilt*,
'frenzy', which has much the same supernatural
connotations in Norse as it has in Irish (De Vries 1962,
170). Particularly suggestive is the word *bjannak*: in *Ynglinga
saga* Ch. 2 Snorri Sturluson says that before Óðinn sent his
men out to battle or on other forays he would lay his hands
on their heads and give them *bjannak*. The best explanation
of this word is that it derives from Irish *beannacht*, itself
derived from Latin *benedictio* 'blessing' (De Vries 1962, 39;
Aðalbjarnarson 1979, I 1). Furthermore, in at least one Irish
source this word, despite its Christian origin, is used in a
remarkably pagan context: in the *Destruction of Dind Ríg* the
dying Cobthach calls his brother Loegaire to him to receive
his *bennach* (Stokes 1891). In the same passage in *Ynglinga
saga* Ch. 2 Snorri also uses an Irish word, *díar*, to denote the
gods (Sveinsson 1957, 4-6; De Vries 1962, 76).

The names of many characters in the sagas betray
Celtic connections: Kjartan, Njáll, Kormákr, the nicknames
feilan, kvaran, bjóla, kamban and so on (Craigie 1897).
Further, it is not true that no saga contains any Irish story or
any Irish hero. *Kjalnesinga saga* contains a garbled version of
the Irish story of Cúchulain's killing of his son, and the
name *Kongofor* in this story appears to be based on that of
legendary king of Ulster, Conchobor (Sveinsson 1957, 15).
In *Egils saga ok Ásmundar* we have an otherworld figure
named Arán, who appears in very much the same context as
the underworld king of the same name in the first branch
of the *Mabinogion* (Chadwick 1957, 174-6). And, of course,
there is the account of the battle of Clontarf at the end of
Njáls saga.

Also, the notion that Old Irish presented an
insuperable barrier to communication is a nonsense.
According to the sagas, several skalds spent a year or more
at the courts of Irish kings (Chadwick 1962, 31). Einar Ól.

Sveinsson has suggested that the unusual skaldic catalectic metres are based directly on Irish metres (1975, 170-217). Gabriel Turville-Petre thought that the *dróttkvætt* stanza itself might show evidence of Irish influence (1972; however Turville-Petre 1976, xxvi-xxviii, while still believing that there is a close relationship between skaldic and Irish poetry, points out "sharp differences" between the the two literatures, differences which Mackenzie 1981 discounts). The similarity of the extremely artificial word-order of the poetry of the Gogynfeirdd (Lloyd-Jones 1948, 6-7) with that of skaldic poetry is also striking. *Laxdæla saga* Ch. 20 tells us that Melkorka, the daughter of an Irish king, taught Irish to her son Ólafr pái. There is a particularly vivid vignette in the Irish account of the Norse invasions concerning the occasional close relations of Viking and Celt. In the elegy for Marthgamain, the brother of Brian Boru murdered by the Norse around 980, the Irish poet states that he cannot condemn the Vikings as he should, because of his close friendship with one of them (Todd 1867, 99; Chadwick 1962, 35). We are told too of a group the Irish chroniclers call the "foreign Gaels", who came from the islands to the north of Ireland, and seem to have been a mixture of Norse and Irish speakers (Chadwick 1962, 26). One could go on. In any case, the supposed language barrier is irrelevant: modern folklore studies have shown that stories cross linguistic borders as if they did not exist (Thompson 1946; Jackson 1961).

Quite simply, the notion that Viking did not and could not have learnt anything from Celt is just not tenable. The instances I have given do not amount to the sort of massive migration of material that Bugge thought he saw. But they are sufficiently varied, and sufficiently widespread, to suggest that Celtic influence might appear at any point in Old Norse. The question then is: how do we identify cases of influence and what do we do with them when we have identifed them? The simplest approach is to equate parallel motifs with direct influence, and then start pursuing parallel motifs through the literature. For example, there are many mists in Celtic stories (e.g. in the *Mabinogion*, Jones 1989, 43) similar to the magic mist that protects Þjóstólfr from his pursuers in *Njáls saga* Ch. 12. The description of Gunnarr, and his trick of swinging a sword so fast it seemed that three swords were in the air at once, in Ch. 19 is very like the epic sword-feats in the *Destruction of Da Derga's Hostel* (Gantz 1981, 94). The remarkable Irish dog that Óláfr pái gives Gunnarr in Ch. 70 has similar guardian powers to those of the hound of Cooley himself, and of many other amazing dogs in Celtic story (e.g. Gantz 1981, 180). As well as the historic and Old Norse literary parallels to the burning of Njáll, one could compare famous Celtic stories about burning people within iron houses: thus in the *Mabinogion* (Jones 1989, 31), in the *Intoxication of the Ulaid* (Gantz 1981, 213) and in the *Destruction of Dind Ríg* (Stokes 1891). A rather closer parallel to these Celtic instances is the burning of the two berserks in *Eyrbyggja saga* Ch. 28 within a specially built house.

This pursuit of parallel motifs, while entertaining, is finally rather fruitless. Even if one accepts these show definite borrowing, just what does this tell us? There may be better ways of approaching the matter of Norse-Celtic links than the proliferation of parallels. Firstly, we might look at just where we find likely Celtic motifs and materials in Old Norse. The distribution of Celtic materials across Old Norse literature is quite uneven. There is very little in the mythological poems of the Poetic Edda which declares itself as possibly Celtic. This is also the case for the poems of the Atli cycle. However, the Sigurðr poems and the three Helgi lays are full of echoes and remniscences of Celtic matter. Turn to the sagas, and we find the same. Certain of the great classical sagas, *Njáls saga* and *Eyrbyggja saga* especially, are rich in Celtic echoes. But others (e.g. *Egils saga*) have very little that could be claimed as Celtic. Indeed, the writings of Snorri Sturluson, dating around 1210 to 1230, are generally free of the possibly Celtic.

Move on to the fourteenth century, into the age of the mythical heroic sagas , and the trickle of Celtic motifs swells to a small stream. In such stories as *Bósa saga*, or *Hjalmpés saga ok Qlvis* or *Halfdanar saga brǫnufostru*, we find much that would be well at home in Celtic stories: giant women who bestow their favours on the hero, and help him in battle and even to marriage (Ellis 1941); much shape-changing: women turning into whales, or birds, or seals, and back again; even sometimes the same boisterous rough humour. Go still later into Icelandic, into the fifteenth century *rímur*, and still more that is Celtic appears (including, incidentally, one of the best analogues I know for *Sir Gawain and the Green Knight* Sveinsson 1957, 11-12; 1975, 117-170). The Celtic elements continue flourish down into modern Icelandic popular tales.

This is really rather odd. Viking and Celt were closest in the Norse kingdom in Ireland which flourished around 850 to 1030. One might expect to find the most Celtic material in the Old Norse literature composed closest to 1030. But the further on in time we get from 1030, up to 1500 at least, the more Celtic material we find in Old Norse.

The best explanation of this was proposed by the great Icelandic scholar Einar Ólafur Sveinsson some thirty years ago. His argument, outlined in his 1957 article "Celtic Elements in Icelandic Tradition", is that this wealth of Celtic stories was brought to Iceland by the Celtic slaves and thralls whom many of the first Norse settlers brought with them. Iceland was built on Irish slaves, just as America was built on Black slaves. Naturally, these slaves and their stories had little prestige, and so one finds little trace of them in the earliest Old Norse literature. But, as the centuries passed their stories dissolved into the mainstream of Norse tradition: their Celtic origins were forgotten, and these stories became part of the common stock.

There is some excellent evidence in favour of this. For instance, the names Njáll and Kormákr: both names are unquestionably Irish, yet neither of the sagas of these two gives any hint of an Irish connection in the families of the heroes. Indeed, *Kormáks saga* is at pains to locate Kormákr's grandfather, also named Kormákr, in Norway around 850. One must conclude that the authors simply were not aware that the names were Irish. Similar are the two late-Eddic poems *Grógaldr* and *Fjǫlsvinnsmál*, probably written in the late 13th century. These are based on the same Celtic story we find in the Welsh *Culhwch ac Olwen* and the Irish *Adventures of Art*, but the poet is so far from being aware that his story is Celtic that he dresses it up, rather incongruously, with all sorts of rags stolen from Norse mythology (Robinson 1991, 229-63, 324, 396). Another example is the great lump of volcanic rock situated beside the Markarfljót river in the south of Iceland, opposite the Eyjafjallajökull. The Norse name for this is *Rauðaskriður*, 'the red slides', named after the characteristic landslips of the red soil on its slopes, and so it is named throughout *Njála*. But its usual name now is *Dímon*, derived from the Irish 'hill with two peaks' (Magnússon 1989, 114), which is exactly what it is. According to Einar Ól. Sveinsson (1954, 92) the name Dímon first appears in a written source in 1363, and since then has driven the other name out: it appears that the Norse had one name for the rock, the Irish another, and eventually the Irish name prevailed.

This argument has a most interesting implication. It suggests that Celtic stories were part of a rich oral tradition of popular story-telling that flourished for centuries after the settlement of Iceland, even though this tradition did not start to make much impact on written literature till around 1300. Evidence for this tradition of story-telling may be found in instances of Celtic versions of international popular tales making their way into the Old Norse area (Christiansen 1959; cf. Almqvist 1978). The tendency of a good deal of modern scholarship is to play down the popular origins of the sagas. Rather, much critical effort has gone into demonstrating that learned, ecclesiastical writing, saints lives and the like, played a vital role in the development of the great classical tradition of the Icelandic saga (e.g Turville-Peter 1953, 142; Hallberg 1962, 67-9; Kristjánsson 1981).

There is another possible view. It is possible that the great sagas grew out of a tradition of popular story-telling. One may put all else aside from the sagas, questions of historicity, source, mutual influence, and see them first as stories. Sagas exist first and foremost in the voice of the author. He or she holds his audience spellbound by an artful arrangement of material, or delights them by a well-turned phrase, or surprises them by a brilliant variation on a worn-out motif. Great literature needs a fertile seedbed, and the Celtic peoples may not have just lent a few motifs to Old Norse, but also may have given their own characteristic fervour, their own delight in story-telling.

What might the Celts have taught the Vikings about story-telling? Firstly, there is what one might call creative freedom. One of the joys of medieval Celtic story-telling is the willingness of the tellers to experiment with new forms of old motifs. No two story-tellers say the same thing in the same way. Consider the amazing islands of the Irish voyage tales, the *Immrama* , dating probably from about 700 AD on. We have islands on single crystal pillars, islands with nets about them, islands with voices booming from the top, islands completely bare except for a single huge plough, islands with giant smiths flinging lumps of red hot metal at the travellers, islands with whole zoos of incredible animals. And islands of women. What women! they come in ones, in nines, in fifties, and with what gifts for the male travellers![1]

Compare versions of the same incident, or incidents, in two or more different sagas, and you find the same phenomenon: like the Celtic storytellers, the saga writers felt free to adapt, to shift the focus, to introduce new characters, to recombine or rearrange incidents. Thus the different accounts of the Norse settlement of North America in *Eiríks saga rauða* and in *Grœnlendinga saga;* even particular incidents such as the death of Guðríðr's husband Þorsteinn are described in radically different ways. Or, look at the different accounts of the death of Þormóðr in *Fóstbrœðra saga* Ch. 24 and in *Heimskringla* (*Óláfs saga ins helga* Ch. 224). Or compare the versions of the wounding of Eyjólfr by Þórdís in *Gísla saga* Ch. 37 and *Eyrbyggja saga* Ch. 13. One could concentrate on what such different versions have in common. This, one might argue, represents a core of historic fact, or it represents the oral formulas which the scribe assembled. Instead, we might look exactly at how such incidents vary. It is precisely there that we will see the individual story- teller at work, exactly as we do in Celtic. It is this spark of creative freedom that transforms the sagas from chronicles to something very different: the difference between *Landnámabók* and *Egils saga*. And this, certainly, is something Celt could have taught Viking.

There are also certain narrative techniques that Viking story-tellers might have learnt from their Celtic counterparts. One finds again and again in the sagas the device of "prospective narrative", or prolepsis. Something is described not as it happens, nor as it has happened, like a flashback in a modern film, but as it will happen: a "flashforward". Most commonly: someone tells a prophecy, or has a dream in which he sees the future. There are splendid instances of this in *Gísla saga*, and in the Eddic poem *Atlamál in Grœnlenzku*. This device of prolepsis is extremely common in Old Irish once again: the seer Cathbad narrates in advance the disastrous life of Deirdre, and Fedelm similarly foretells Cúchulain's triumph over Medb's forces. It is worth pointing out, I think, that one finds virtually no instances of "flashback" in either Old Norse or medieval Celtic literature, but there are scores, perhaps hundreds, of instances of this "flashforward". By contrast, modern films and novels use flashback extensively, but flashforward hardly at all.

Also, there is a highly distinctive variation on this "flashforward" device which we find in both Old Norse and Celtic. This variation is the description of a prospective enemy. In chapter 63 of *Laxdœla saga* Helgi Harðbeinsson, after taking part in the killing of Bolli, asks his servant to describe to him each person in the band of men coming to attack him in vengeance. The servant describes each in detail; then Helgi names each man from the description and comments on each man. (The dialogue in *Njála* at the Althing, where each chieftain looks at Skarpheðinn and asks who is that menacing looking fellow with the sardonic smile, looks like another variant of this trick.) Again, this technique of the description of a prospective enemy is widespread in Celtic literature: it is found in *Branwen*, in the *Táin*, in *Fled Bricrend* and is used to astonishing effect in *Da Derga's Hostel*. Here are just a few story-telling devices Viking may have learnt from Celt; further exploration could turn up many more.

I do not suggest that Old Norse story-telling is a pale shadow of Celtic story-telling, or that the Icelandic sagas are inferior versions of Irish ones. Consider the description of Cúchulain in his war fury as he prepares for battle, in the *Táin*. His body twists inside its skin so that his feet and shins and knees face to the back and his heels and calves face to the front. The sinews of his neck stretch and swell into knobs, each as big as a baby's head. His mouth peels wide open so that you can see his lungs and liver flapping in his throat. Flames spurt from his head. His hair boils into stiff spikes of rage, and finally "tall and thick, steady and strong, high as the mast of a noble ship, rose up from the dead centre of his skull a straight spout of black blood." (Kinsella 1969, 150-3).

There is nothing in Old Norse like this. A comparison of Celtic and Viking helps us reach an appreciation of the native strengths of eaCh. Broadly, Celtic literature, all the way from the *Táin* up to *Finnegans Wake*, is much stronger in detail than in structure. Stories tend to be frameworks for the glittering ornaments of their author's fantasy. Further, the Ireland and Wales of Celtic story, for all their placenames, are lands poets have imagined. Historians are helpless in them. Occasionally, something logical happens – but only occasionally.

Not so the classic sagas. Firstly, they are rooted in the workaday, the particular: in the yearly round of harvest, feastings and famines. Occasionally they trip into the fantastic, but the usual world always returns. Secondly, the finest sagas are much more than collections of happenings, or strings of incidents. There is a formal beauty about *Njáls saga* and *Egils saga*: incident balances, echoes or foreshadows incident; there is contrast and development of character; sequence calls to sequence across the whole length of the saga.

Such art does not come from nothing. What has survived of early Icelandic literature gives us imperfect glimpses of what preceded the great sagas: the rather rudimentary *Fóstbrœðra* and *Grœnlendinga* sagas; saints and kings lives. As well as this, I suggest that the sagas grew out of a tradition of popular story-telling. This tradition is known to us, indirectly, through various references in the sagas. But we can also know it more directly: I suggest that vital to this tradition were the stories, and the delight in telling them, brought to Iceland by the Celtic slaves of the first settlers. Hence, a reading of Celtic literature can provide an unexpected glimpse of the origins of the sagas.

The question of "what Celt taught Viking" might be better rephrased to "what Celt can teach the student of Old

Norse". Rather than answer that, I will make a few
recommendations. Read James Delargy's classic Rhys lecture
of 1945, *The Gaelic Storyteller*. Here is Delargy on the essence
of story-telling: "It draws the breath of life from the lips of
men and from the applause of an appreciative fireside
audience" (1945, 13). A fiction, if you like, but one told by a
real teller to a real audience. Then read the *Cattle Raid of
Cooley* and the *Mabinogion*, in the splendid translations of
Thomas Kinsella, and Gwyn Jones and Thomas Jones. If
nothing else, just read the first few pages of *Culhwch ac
Olwen*. Such stories as these preserve the past; they enchant
the present; they unlock the future. The Celtic story-teller
knew that. So did the Icelandic story-teller.

Further reading

Good introductory surveys of the interaction of Viking and
Celt are to be found in Ó Cuív 1962, Chadwick 1957 and
Sveinsson 1957. Andersson 1964, 56-61 provides a more
cautionary note, while the two 1982 articles by Sims-
Williams attach stringent conditions on belief in any type of
borrowing between any two literatures. Sigurðsson 1988
covers the widest range of material while Chesnutt and
Erlingsson give a full bibliography of materials up to 1970.
A sense of the popular tale materials which may underlie
much surviving Old Norse and medieval Celtic literature
can be derived from Jackson 1961 and Delargy 1945. There
are some excellent translations of medieval Celtic materials:
beside those mentioned in the last paragraph, both Jackson
1971 and Gantz 1981 are readily available.

Bibliography

Aðalbjarnarson, B. 1979. (ed.) *Heimskringla*. Vols I-III.
        Íslenzk fornrit XXVI-VIII. Reyjkjavík.
Almqvist, B. 1978. "Scandinavian and Celtic Folklore
        Contacts in the Earldom of Orkney". *Saga
        Book* XX, 80-105.
Andersson, T.M. 1964. *The Problem of Icelandic Saga Origins*.
        Yale.

Bugge, S. 1899. *The Home of the Eddic Poems.* London. (Tr. L. Schofield).

Chadwick, N.K. 1957. "Literary Tradition in the Old Norse and Celtic World". *Saga Book* XIV, 164-199.

Chadwick, N.K. 1962. "The Vikings and the Western World". In Ó Cuív 1962, 13-42.

Chesnutt, M. and Erlingsson, D. 1970-2. "Norse-Celtic Bibliographical Survey". *Mediaeval Scandinavia* 3-5.

Christiansen, R. Th. 1959. *Studies in Irish and Scandinavian Folktales.* Copenhagen.

Clover, C. J. and Lindow, J. 1985. (eds.) *Old Norse-Icelandic Literature: A Critical Guide.* Islandica XLV. Ithaca.

Craigie, W. A. 1897. "Gaelic Words and Names in the Icelandic Sagas". *Zeitschrift für celtische Philologie* I, 439-54.

Cross, T. P. and Slover, C.H. 1935. (trans.) *Ancient Irish Tales.* Chicago.

Delargy, J. 1945. (= S. Ó Dúilearga.) *The Gaelic Storyteller.* Sir John Rhys Memorial Lecture. London.

De Vries, J. 1962. *Altnordisches etymylogisches Wörterbuch.* Leiden. (2nd Ed.)

Ellis, H.R. 1941. "Fostering by Giants in Old Norse Saga Literature". *Medium Aevum* 10, 70-85.

Gantz, J. 1981. *Early Irish Myths and Sagas.* Harmondsworth.

Hallberg, P. 1962. *The Icelandic Saga.* Lincoln. (Trans. P. Schach)

Jackson, K. H. 1961. *The International Popular Tale in Early Welsh Tradition.* Cardiff. (Gregynog Lectures.)

Jackson, K. H. 1962. "The Celtic Languages during the Viking Period". In Ó Cuív 1962, 3-11.

Jackson, K. H. 1971. *A Celtic Miscellany.* Harmondsworth.

Jones, G. and Jones , T. (trans.) 1989. *The Mabinogion.* London.

Kinsella, T. (trans.) 1969. *The Táin.* Dublin.

Kristjánsson, J. 1981. "Learned style or saga style?". In *Speculum Norrœnum,* 260-92.

Lloyd-Jones, J. 1948. *The Court Poetry of the Welsh Princes.* Sir John Rhys Memorial Lecture.

Mackenzie, B. Gordon. 1981. "On the Relation of Norse
    Skaldic verse to Irish Syllabic Poetry". In
    Speculum Norrœnum, 337-56.
Magnússon, Ásgeir Blöndal. 1989. *Íslenzk orðsifjabók*.
    Reykjavík.
Ó Cuív, B. 1962. *The Impact of the Scandinavian Invasions
    on the Celtic-speaking People*. Dublin (reissued
    1975).
Richards, M. 1962. "Norse Place-names in Wales". In Ó Cuív
    1962, 51-60.
Robinson, P.M.W. 1991. "An Edition of *Svipdagsmál*".
    Unpublished D.Phil Thesis. Oxford.
Sigurðsson, Gísli. 1988. *Gaelic Influence in Iceland*. Studia
    Islandica 46. Reykjavík.
Sims-Williams, P. 1982a. "The Evidence for Vernacular Irish
    Influences on Early Medieval Welsh
    Literature". In *Ireland in Medieval Europe
    (Hughes Memorial Studies)*. Ed. D. Whitelock et
    al. Cambridge, 235-57.
Sims-Williams, P. 1982b. "The Significance of the Irish
    Personal Names in Culhwch ac Olwen".
    Bulletin of the Board of Celtic Studies XXIX, 600-
    20.
*Speculum Norrœnum: Norse Sudies in Memory of Gabriel Turville-
    Petre*. Ed. U.M. Dronke et al. Oxford, 1981.
Stokes, W. 1891. "The Destruction of Dind Ríg". *Zeitschrift
    für celtische Philologie* III, 1-14.
Sveinsson, Einar Ól. 1954. *Brennu-Njáls saga*. Íslenzk fornrit
    XII. Reyjkjavík.
Sveinsson, Einar Ól. 1957. "Celtic Elements in Icelandic
    Tradition", *Béaloideas* XXV, 3-24.
Sveinsson, Einar Ól. 1975. *Löng er för*. Studia Islandica 34.
    Reykjavík.
Thompson, S. 1946. *The Folktale*. Berkeley.
Todd, J.H. 1867. *The War of the Gaedhil with the Gaill*.
    London.
Turville-Petre, E.O.G. 1953. *Origins of Icelandic Literature*.
    Oxford.
Turville-Petre, E.O.G. 1972. "*Dróttkvætt* and Irish Syllabic
    Measures". In *Nine Norse Studies*. London, 154-
    80.

Turville-Petre, E.O.G. 1976. *Scaldic Poetry*. Oxford.

1   This paragraph is a conflation of material from the *Immrama* of Maeldúin, Hui Corra, Bran, Snedgus and *Navigatio Brendani*.

Egils saga and Njáls saga: bibliographical guides

John Hines

General note
This section is intended to form a selective guide to published texts and studies of these two sagas. Although far from exhaustive, it is hoped that it will give an accurate and informative impression of the volume of work in particular fields, and of the range of topics that relatively modern scholarship in particular has been concerned with. While seeking to cater primarily for the English-speaking student — as, for instance, in the notes on Modern English translations of these sagas — I have sought not to obscure the fact that a great deal of the important literature on these sagas is written in the modern Scandinavian languages and in German. A key to abbreviated titles of periodicals and collections of essays that are referred to more than once in the bibliography appears at the end. Some publishers' names are also abbreviated.

Egils saga
Egils saga, sometimes referred to by the Icelandic diminutive *Egla*, is preserved in what can be called full-length versions in two 14th-century manuscripts (*Möðruvallabók* and *Wolfenbüttelbók*) and one 17th-century copy of a 14th-century manuscript (*Ketilsbók*). There are several further fragments of medieval manuscript copies of the saga, of which a fragment known as ϑ (theta) is especially important, as it dates back to the middle of the 13th century: it is the earliest evidence of the saga that we have, and was perhaps written not long after the saga was composed. The usual status and dating of this fragment have, however, very recently been challenged by Ólafur Halldórsson, 'Nema skyld nauðsyn banni', in *Lygisögur sagðar Sverri Tómassyni fimmtugum 5. apríl 1991* (Reykjavík, 1991), 73-7.

The standard modern edition of *Egils saga* is that of
Sigurður Nordal, volume II in the *Íslenzk Fornrit* series, first
published in 1933. This followed the version of the saga in
the Möðruvallabók manuscript, which is dated to the period
1316-1350 and is thus the earliest of the full-length versions.
The most substantial discrepancy between Nordal's edition
and this manuscript version lies in the provision of full texts
of Egill's three known long poems, *Hǫfuðlausn*, *Sonatorrek*
and *Arinbjarnarkviða*, where they fit in the saga, though the
Möðruvallabók version contains only a text of
Arinbjarnarkviða, and that as a later addition. More of these
poems are given in the other early full-length versions of
the saga, but Nordal's — and other — editions of the poems
have to draw on other manuscript sources, and quotations
in Snorri Sturluson's *Edda*, too. Some works on Egill's
poetry are noted later in this bibliography; see also
Carolyne Larrington's essay on *Sonatorrek* and
Arinbjarnarkviða in this book.

Nordal's introduction to his edition of the saga gives a
full account of its manuscript tradition. It also discusses,
and promotes, certain topics in the study of the saga. There
is particular emphasis on the literary and historical sources
and relations of the saga, and a discussion of the suggestion
that Snorri Sturluson might be the author of *Egils saga*. A
general commentary on the saga that can be compared with
Nordal's work, especially in respect of the elucidation of the
skaldic verses, is Halldór Halldórsson's *Egluskýringar handa
skólum* (Bókaforlag Þorsteins M. Jónssonar h.f., 1950).

Egils saga has been translated into Modern English
several times: there are three relatively recent versions to be
especially recommended. Gwyn Jones's *Egil's Saga* (Syracuse
University Press, 1960) provides an introduction with the
translation, discussing a similar range of topics to those
covered by Nordal's introduction, with particular emphasis
on the theme of kingship and on Egill's contrarious
character; there are also notes. Christine Fell's *Egils Saga*
(Dent, 1975) also has a good introduction of similar range
and length, together with a select bibliography, notes, and
useful indexes of personal and place-names. Hermann
Pálsson and Paul Edwards' *Egil's Saga* (Penguin Classics,

1976) has a shorter introduction, and a similarly useful glossary of characters in the saga.

The proposition that Snorri Sturluson was the author of *Egils saga* can be traced back to the early 19th century, but along with Nordal's discussion, modern study of the question can start with Peter Hallberg's *Snorri Sturluson och Egils saga Skalla-Grímssonar. Ett forsök till språklig författarbestämning* (StI 20, 1962), in Swedish but with a full English summary. This book superseded earlier major studies by Per Wieselgren, *Författarskapet till Eigla* (Lund, 1927) and M. C. van den Toorn, *Zur Verfasserfrage der Egilssaga Skallagrímssonar* (Böhlau, 1959), whose arguments Hallberg summarizes and criticises. From a close comparative study of diction in *Egils saga* and *Heimskringla*, Hallberg concludes that Snorri was the author of *Egils saga*. See further Peter Hallberg, 'Íslendinga Saga och Egla, Laxdœla, Eyrbyggja, Njála, Grettla. Ett språktest', *MM* 1965(3-4), 89-106. Vésteinn Ólason gives a good summary of the issues in 'Er Snorri höfundur Egils sögu?', *Sk* 142 (1968), 48-67. Hallberg's conclusion that Snorri was the author was supported by further work by Ralph West, 'Snorri Sturluson and *Egils Saga*: Statistics of Style', *SS* LII (1980), 163-93, though he qualified this with the proposition that the *Egils saga* we have is a composite work, with a second hand particularly evident at the end of the saga. Sveinn Bergsveinsson, 'Tveir höfundar Egils sögu', *Sk* 157 (1983), 99-116, also argues for composite authorship.

Studies of the diction of *Egils saga* that consider the function of formulae rather the question of authorship are those of Heinrich Beck, 'Erzählhaltung und Quellenberufung in der *Egils saga*', *Skand* 3(2) (1973), 89-102, and L. Michael Bell, 'Oral Allusion in Egils saga Skalla-Grímssonar. A Computer-Aided Approach', *ANF* 91 (1976), 51-65, and 'Fighting words in *Egils saga*: Lexical pattern as standard-bearer', *ANF* 95 (1980), 89-112.

Much has been published on the relationships between *Egils saga* and other known texts, especially *Landnámabók*. Björn M. Ólsen's 'Landnáma og Egils saga', *Aarbøger for nordisk Oldkyndighed og Historie* Series 2 no.19 (1904), 167-247, is a detailed and fundamental study. More recent is Bjarni Einarsson's *Litterære forudsætninger for Egils saga* (Stofnun Árna Magnússonar, 1975), which offers a broad conspectus of the saga's literary relationships, with *konungasögur* (Kings' sagas) as well as with *Landnámabók*, with *Orkneyinga saga*, and with other skalds' sagas, and an important discussion of the medieval concepts of history and fiction in relation to these works. Jónas Kristjánsson's 'Egils saga og Konungasögur' of 1977, *SR*, 449-72, also gives a detailed and systematic review of the topic: this study ends by noting the possibility of the composition of the saga late in Snorri's life, *circa* 1240. Also to be mentioned are further discussions by T. M. Andersson in his *The Problem of Icelandic Saga Origins* (YUP, 1964), 83-95 and 123-8; Anne Holtsmark, 'Skallagrims Heimamenn', *MM* 1971(3-4), 97-105; Bjarni Einarsson, 'Fólgið fé á Mosfelli', *SR* (1977), 100-6; and Alfred Jakobsen, 'Om parallellepisoder i Egils saga', *Edda* LXXXV (1985), 315-8.

Studies of the structure of *Egils saga* are all more or less concurrently explorations of inferred meanings, morals or purposes of the work such as have already been noted in connection with introductions to editions or translations of the saga. General views of the saga by Jan de Vries, *Altnordische Literaturgeschichte* (Walter de Gruyter, 1941-42), 297-304, and Peter Hallberg, *The Icelandic Saga* (UNP, 1962), 27-8 and 125-31, fall very much into this category. T. M. Andersson's *The Icelandic Family Saga. An Analytic Reading* (HUP, 1967) concentrates on the structural study of these sagas, and interprets *Egils saga* (pp.97-110) primarily in terms of the study of character, and of kingship as a theme. Vésteinn Ólason's recent 'Jorvik Revisited — with Egil Skalla Grimsson', *Northern Studies* 27 (1990), 64-76, is interesting in that it briefly but concisely puts the case that Egill's meeting with Eiríkr in York settles the theme of kingship in the saga, disrupting unity in the work as the remainder of the saga switches to biography. Jan Sand Sørensen's 'Komposition og Værdiunivers i Egils Saga', *Gr* IV (1980), 260-72, also interprets the structure of the saga in social and individualistic terms, seeing the saga as, in effect, a political *exemplum* on the need for subordinacy, focussed on contrasting characters within Egill's family rather than on kings. On the topic of kingship, see further Hermann Pálsson 'Um kærleikann í Egils sögu' in A. Kristjánsson *et al.*

eds., *Afmælisrit til Dr.Phil. Steingríms J. Þorsteinssonar Prófessors* (Reykjavík, 1971), 59-62.

Egill as a character not surprisingly attracts much interest. On the question of his heroism there is T. M. Andersson, 'The Displacement of the Heroic Ideal in the Family Sagas', *Speculum* 45 (1970), 575-93, reprinted in *Sagas* (1989), 40-70, and Preben Meulengracht Sørensen, 'Starkaðr, Loki and Egill Skallagrímsson', *Sagas* (1989), 146-59, a translation of the paper that had appeared in *SR* (1977), 759-68. Further on the Starkaðr model, there is Kaaren Grimstad, 'The Giant as a Heroic Model: the Case of Egill and Starkaðr', *SS* 48 (1976), 284-98. On Egill as a lover (cf. Alison Finlay, this volume) there is a brief paper by Eysteinn Þorvaldsson, 'Hugleiðingar um ástarsögu Egils', *Mímir* 13(2) (1968), 20-4.

But it is Egill as a poet, and correspondingly *Egils saga* as a study of poetry, that is particularly intensely studied. Focussing on Egill as poet, although moving in very different directions, are studies by Hallvard Lie, 'Jorvikferden. Et vendepunkt i Egil Skallagrimssons liv', *Edda* XLVI (1947), 145-248 (a rambling piece), Kristján Albertsson, 'Egill Skallagrímsson í Jórvík', *Sk* 150 (1976), 88-98, Margaret Clunies Ross, 'The Art of Poetry and the Figure of the Poet in *Egils saga*', *Parergon* 22 (1978), 3-12, reprinted in *Sagas* (1989), 126-45, and Laurence de Looze, 'Poet, Poem and Poetic Process in *Egils Saga Skalla-Grímssonar*', *ANF* 104 (1989), 123-42. Deservedly influential still is Sigurður Nordal's 'Átrúnaður Egils Skallagrímssonar', *Sk* 98 (1924), 145-65, an exploration of Egill's paganism, especially as reflected in his poetry. A. C. Bouman, 'Egill Skallagrímsson's Poem *Sonatorrek*', in *Patterns* (1962), 17-40, and Bo Ralph, 'Om tillkomsten av *Sonatorrek*', *ANF* 91 (1976), 153-65, focus on Egill's highly personal elegy *Sonatorrek* in literary-historical and biographical terms. *Sonatorrek* itself attracts greatest interest amongst Egill's poems. There are informative editions by Ólafur M. Ólafsson, 'Sonatorrek', *Av* NF X (1968), 133-200, and Gabriel Turville-Petre, 'The Sonatorrek', in G. Turville-Petre and J. S. Martin eds., *Iceland and the Medieval World. Studies in Honour of Ian Maxwell* (1974), 33-55, the latter reappearing in Turville-Petre's *Scaldic Poetry* (Oxford University Press, 1976), 24-41. Both these works of Turville-Petre's contain further valuable study and notes on other poetry of Egill's. M. C. van den Toorn's critical appreciation, 'Egils Sonatorrek als dichterische Leistung', *Zeitschrift für deutsche Philologie* 77 (1958), 46-59, should also be noted. On *Hǫfuðlausn*, there is Odd Nordland's *Hǫfuðlausn i Egils saga. Ein tradisjonkritisk studie* (Det Norske Samlaget, 1956), a work of considerably wider scope than its main title would suggest. Most study has concentrated on the historical circumstances of this poem: see, for instance, Gwyn Jones, 'Egill Skallagrímsson in England' (British Academy: Sir Israel Gollancz Memorial Lecture, 1952) and on the date of the poem, Jón Helgason, 'Hǫfuðlausnarhjal', in *Einarsbók. Afmæliskveðja til Einars Ól. Sveinssonar* (Reykjavík, 1969), 156-76, with a response from Dietrich Hofmann, 'Das Reimwort *giǫr* in Egill Skallagrímssons *Hǫfuðlausn*', *MS* 6 (1973), 91-101.

Njáls saga
Njáls saga, often referred to by the Icelandic diminutive *Njála*, has the strongest medieval manuscript tradition of all the Icelandic family sagas, with 19 different vellum manuscript copies dated from *circa* 1300 to 1550 preserved at least in part, and many later manuscript copies. Einar Ólafur Sveinsson based his Íslenzk Fornrit edition of the saga (volume XII, 1954) on the 14th-century Möðruvallabók text — also the source of the standard edition of *Egils saga* (see above) — although this manuscript lacks chapters 1-29. Previous editions had been based on the nearly complete Reykjabók text, dated to *circa* 1300, and thus thought to be relatively close to the date of the composition of the saga, which Sveinsson (e.g. *op.cit.*, lxxv-lxxxiv) places about 1280-1285. The fundamental study of the manuscripts of *Njáls saga* is Einar Ól. Sveinsson's *Studies in the Manuscript Tradition of Njálssaga* (StI 13, 1953).

Two quite recent Modern English translations of the saga are Carl F. Bayerschmidt and Lee M. Hollander's *Njál's Saga* (New York University Press, 1955), with a concise introduction and notes, and Magnus Magnusson and

Hermann Pálsson's *Njal's Saga* (Penguin Classics, 1960), which also offers a brief introduction, and useful genealogical tables and a glossary of names. An early translation of the saga, George Webbe Dasent's *The Story of Burnt Njal* (Edmonton and Douglas, Edinburgh, 1861), is an attractive and impressive product of Victorian scholarship in this field, with a two-hundred-page preface and introduction on the historical context of the tale, further historical appendices, a full index, maps and figures. This fine translation has been reprinted several times, *inter alia* as the Everyman's Library (J.M.Dent & Sons) version of the saga (now out of print), although with much of the additional material omitted.

Njáls saga is arguably the best known, and certainly the most extensively studied, of the Old Icelandic sagas. Several books have been written devoted to this saga. A leader in this field was Einar Ól. Sveinsson, the editor of the saga, most notably with his book *Á Njálsbúð Bók um mikið listaverk* (Hið Íslenzka Bókmenntafélag, 1943), which is translated into English, with a critical introduction, by Paul Schach, and published as *Njáls saga: A Literary Masterpiece* (UNP, 1971). At the heart of this book, as in first place in Sveinsson's introduction to his edition, is some inspired response to the major characters of the saga; other major topics discussed in both places by Einar Ól. Sveinsson are the sources, art and structure of the saga, and its moral perspective.   Richard F. Allen's *Fire and Iron. Critical Approaches to Njáls saga* (University of Pittsburgh Press, 1971) concentrates on structure, form and style in the saga, noting separate shaping forces amongst which literate and oral traditions are major detectable factors.   Lars Lönnroth's *Njáls saga. A critical introduction* (UCP, 1976) also analyses the saga as the product of traditional material processed by the clerical mind in the social context of late 13th-century Iceland. To appreciate the impact of this book, one should look at the adverse reviews of it by Peter Foote, 'New Dimensions in "Njáls Saga"', *Scandinavica* 18(1) (1979), 49-58, and Rory McTurk, *SB* XX(1-2) (1978-9), 145-50, and a more favourable one by Christine Fell in *MS* 10 (1977), 189-91.   Amongst other works attempting a comprehensive view of the meaning of the saga, one should note Peter Hallberg's *The Icelandic Saga* (UNP, 1962), 131-6, where it is discussed as a tragedy of fate, and his 'Njáls Saga — en medeltida moralitet?', *ScI* 24 (1973), 3-14, which again focusses very much on character. Alan J. Berger's 'The Meaning of *Njáls saga*', *Skand* 11(1), 1-8, is strangely short and inconclusive.

The possible identity of the author of *Njáls saga* has been discussed at length in Modern Icelandic. Barði Guðmundsson collected together arguments from several papers of his from the late 1930's to the earlier 1950's in *Höfundur Njálu* (BM, 1958), arguing for the authorship of one Þorvarðr Þórarinsson. This view was rejected by Einar Ól. Sveinsson (e.g. in his edition, c-cxii); the arguments on both sides were surveyed by Gunnar Benediktsson in 'Staðhæfing gegn staðhæfingu', *Tímarit Máls og Menningar* 26 (1965), 186-208. The question has most recently been taken up again by Hermann Pálsson in *Uppruni Njálu og hugmyndir* (BM: Íslenzk Ritskýring 1, 1984), 97-112, where Barði Guðmundsson's arguments are swiftly rejected, and the strength of the case for the authorship of Bishop Árni Þorláksson of Skálholt is advanced.

Extensive indeed is the work on the literary relations of *Njáls saga.* On the whole these relations emerge as forming a mosaic of relatively small-scale echoes, survivals or borrowings from other identifiable literary works rather than any thorough-going dependence or assimilation. This pattern is well represented by the developed notes that make up most of Hermann Pálsson's *Uppruni Njálu og hugmyndir* (see above). The question of relationship between *Njáls saga* and *Laxdœla saga* is a persistent one, on which see T. M. Andersson, *The Problem of Icelandic Saga Origins* (YUP, 1964), 95-103, and Heimir Pálsson, 'Rittengsl Laxdælu og Njálu', *Mímir* 11(2) (1967), 5-16. The deepest literary-historical echoes have been discovered by George Clark, '*Beowulf* and *Njáls saga*', in Peter Foote *et al.* eds., *Proceedings of the First International Saga Conference, University of Edinburgh, 1971* (VS, 1973), 66-87, and Carol J. Clover, 'Hildigunnr's Lament', in J. Lindow *et al.* eds. *Structure and Meaning in Old Norse Literature. New Approaches to Textual Analysis and Literary Criticism* (Odense University Press,

1986), 141-83, both of them essays that can be strongly recommended. Amongst studies dealing with closer literary parallels and sources should be noted Denton Fox, '*Njáls Saga* and The Western Literary Tradition', *Comparative Literature* XV(4) (1963), 289-310, Thomas D. Hill, 'The Evisceration of Bróðir in *Brennu-Njáls Saga*', *Traditio* XXXVII (1981), 437-44, Alfred Jakobsen, 'Njáls saga og Selsbanetåtten', *ANF* 99 (1984), 126-30, and Hermann Pálsson, 'Í Gunnarshaugi', *Sk* 163 (1989), 330-46.

As with *Egils saga*, there are few studies of the structure and style of *Njáls saga* that are not at the same time studies of the function of these features and therefore, in effect, interpretations of the saga. Less 'applied' studies of style in this way are Walter Scheps, 'Historicity and Oral Narrative in *Njáls saga*', *SS* 46(2) (1974), 120-33 and Lars Lönnroth's 'Structural Divisions in the Njála Manuscripts', *ANF* 90 (1975), 49-79, both of which ultimately emphasize the 'literary' nature of *Njáls saga*, and Ingegerd Fries's 'Njals saga 700 år senare', *ScI* 32 (1981), 30-54. Concerned with the general structure of the saga and its interpretation are T. M. Andersson, *The Icelandic Family Saga* (HUP, 1967), 291-307; Oskar Bandle, 'Strukturprobleme in der Njáls saga', in Oskar Bandle *et al.* eds. *Festschrift für Siegfried Gütenbrunner* (Carl Winter, 1972), 1-14, a concise but remarkably comprehensive summary; and more selectively but no less effectively, Constance Hieatt, 'Hrútr's Voyage to Norway and the Structure of *Njála*', *Journal of English and Germanic Philology* 77 (1978), 484-94, reprinted in *Sagas* (1989), 272-80. I. R. Maxwell's 'Pattern in *Njáls Saga*', *SB* XV(1-2) (1959), 17-47, argues for the final unity or coherency of the saga; this is a topic also discussed by Carol J. Clover, in connection with what would appear to be the most blatant digression in the saga, in 'Open Composition: The Atlantic Interlude in *Njáls saga*', in *Sagas* (1989), 280-92, abstracted from her book *The Medieval Saga* (Cornell University Press, 1982). Focussing on the moral effects of more localized aspects of style are Lars Lönnroth, 'Rhetorical Persuasion in the Sagas', *SS* 42(2) (1970), 157-89, W. F. Bolton, 'The Njála Narrator and the Picture Plane', *SS* 44(2) (1972), 186-209, and Paul Beekman Taylor, 'Wielders and Wasters of Words: Bare Lies and Garnished

Truths in *Njáls saga*', in R. Simek *et al.* eds. *Sagnaskemmtun.*
Studies in Honour of Hermann Pálsson (HBN, 1986), 287-96.
Following the artistic rather than the moral effect of
technique at this level is Peter Hallberg's 'Några
anteckningar om replik och dialog i Njals saga', in Kurt
Rudolph *et al.* eds., *Festschrift Walter Baetke* (HBN, 1966), 130-
50.

In a very general way, the most persistent feature in
critical understanding of *Njáls saga* is an interpretation of
the saga as a vehicle for the comparative examination of
traditional, heroic ethics, in which the concept of 'honour'
is a major factor, against broadly contrasting, medieval
Christian ideals. This division is clearly presented in Oskar
Bandle's article (as noted above). On traditional moral
attitudes, see Nanna Ólafsdóttir, 'Nokkur
menningarsöguleg dæmi úr Njálu', *Sk* 151 (1977), 59-72.
Carola L. Gottzmann, *Njáls saga. Rechtsproblematik im Dienste*
sozio-kultureller Deutung (Peter Lang: Europäische
Hochschulschriften Reihe 1 Bd.577, 1982), studies the legal
and social institutions portrayed in *Njáls saga* exhaustively in
these terms. On the issue of feud, see William Ian Miller,
'The Central Feud in *Njáls saga*', *Sagas* (1989), 293-322, a
slightly revised version of the author's 'Justifying
Skarpheðinn: Of Pretext and Politics in the Icelandic
Bloodfeud', *SS* 55(4) (1983), 316-44, and Jesse L. Byock,
Feud in the Icelandic Saga (UCP, 1982), especially pp.161-90.
Lars Lönnroth, 'The Noble Heathen: A Theme in the
Sagas', *SS* 41(1), 1-29, looks at the Christian-pagan
dichotomy at the level of character, and with reference to
the concept of 'heroism'. See also Peter Hallberg, *The*
Icelandic Saga (as above), 110-3, and Robert Cook, 'The
effect of the conversion in *Njáls saga*', in *Preprints of the*
Eighth International Saga Conference (Göteborg Universität,
1991), 94-102, on pagan and Christian characters, and
George Clark, '*Beowulf* and *Njáls saga*' (as above) on
Skarpheðinn.

Closely involved with the recurrent topic of 'character'
are the issues of gender and sexuality. A number of papers
on this topic that appeared quite close together are Helga
Kress, 'Ekki hǫfu vér kvennaskap. Nokkrar laustengdar
athuganir um karlmennsku og kvenhatur í Njálu', in *SR*

(1977), 293-313, reprinted in Norwegian as 'Manndom og Misogyni. Noen refleksjoner omkring kvinnesynet i Njåls saga', *Gardar* X (1979), 35-51, a wide-ranging survey of conventional gender attitudes; Marina Mundt, 'Kvinnens forhold til ekteskapet i Njåls saga', *Edda* LXXVI(1/2) (1976), 17-25, a straightforward, inductive analysis of women's expectations and experiences in marriage; and Ursula Dronke, *The Role of Sexual Themes in Njáls saga* (VS: Dorothea Coke Memorial Lecture in Northern Studies, 1980) — cf. Heather O'Donoghue, this volume. A. C. Bouman, 'Literature and Myth, the picture of Hallgerðr Hǫskuld's daughter', in *Patterns* (1962), 3-13, offers a straightforward summary of Hallgerðr as a character.

Of the verses within *Njáls saga*, *Darraðarljóð*, a poem associated with the Battle of Clontarf in Ireland on Good Friday 1014, attracts particular interest. An important article is Anne Holtsmark's '«Vefr Darraðar»', *MM* 1939, 74-96, explaining details of the poem in terms of the weaving techniques that form its basic conceit, and offering a study of the term *darraðr*. Russell Poole's more recent 'Darraðarljóð 2: ǫrum hrælaðr', *MM* 1985(1-2), 87-94, offers a further reading of a detail in the poem in the same technical terms, and also provides a useful bibliography.

A general survey of recent topics of *Njáls saga* study with a bibliography is provided by Jan Ragnar Hagland in 'Njáls saga i 1970- og 1980-åra. Eit oversyn over nyare forskning', *ScI* 38 (1987), 36-50.

Abbreviations
ANF   *Arkiv för Nordisk Filologi*
Av   *Andvari*
BM   Bókaútgáfa Menningarsjóðs
Gr   *Gripla*
HBN   Hermann Böhlaus Nachfolger
HUP   Harvard University Press
MM   *Maal og Minne*
MS   *Mediaeval Scandinavia*
Patterns (1962) A. C. Bouman, *Patterns in Old English and Old Icelandic Literature* (Universitaire Pers Leiden:

Leidse Germanistische en Anglistische Reeks, 1, 1962).

Sagas (1989)   John Tucker ed., *Sagas of the Icelanders. A Book of Essays* (Garland, 1989).

SB   *Saga-Book*

ScI   *Scripta Islandica*

Sk   *Skírnir*

Skand   *Skandinavistik*

SR (1977)   Einar G. Pétursson et al. eds., *Sjötíu Ritgerðir helgaðar Jakobi Benediktssyni 20. júlí 1977* (Stofnun Árna Magnússonar, 1977).

SS   *Scandinavian Studies*

StI   Studia Islandica

UCP   University of California Press

UNP   University of Nebraska Press

VS   The Viking Society for Northern Research

YUP   Yale University Press